MPHO SALEMANE PHATUDI

MARRIAGE
Repackaged

Marriage Repackaged
First Edition, First Impression 2020
ISBN: 978-1-990961-30-4
Copyright © Mpho Salemane Phatudi

Published by:
Inspired Publishing
PO Box 82058 | Southdale | 2135
Johannesburg, South Africa

Email: info@inspiredpublishing.co.za
www.inspiredpublishing.co.za

© All rights are reserved. Apart from any fair dealing for the purpose of research, criticism or review as permitted under the Copyright Act, no part of this publication may be reproduced, stored in a retrieval system or transmitted, in any form or by any means, electronic, mechanical, photocopying, recording, or otherwise, without the prior written permission of the copyright holder.

MARRIAGE
Repackaged

TABLE OF CONTENTS

Marriage Repackaged Extract	1
Acknowlegements	5
Preface	7
Chapter One: The State Of Consciousness	11
Chapter Two: The Enemy Within And Among Us	19
Chapter Three: Violence In A Relationship	26
Chapter Four: Healing Oneself	30
Chapter Five: Waiting On God	42
Chapter Six: The Divine Love Of God	55
Chapter Seven: Acceptance Of Your Reality	60
Chapter Eight: The Truth About Creation	65
Chapter Nine: Understanding Humanity And What We Are Made Up Of	81
Chapter Ten: Understanding Freedom: Gods Perspective	89
Chapter Eleven: Discovering The Authentic Self And Understanding The Power Of One	95
Chapter Twelve: Advanced Healing Mechanism	99
Chapter Thirteen: Spiritual Maturity	121
Chapter Fourteen: The Spirit Of Christ	126
Epilogue	148

Marriage Repackaged Extract

by Mpho Salemane Phatudi; published by Inspired Publishing;
ISBN : 9781990961304

Marriage Repacked is a self-healing book based on the ancient knowledge and the origin of Man and God/Creator/All That Is's original purpose regarding relationships. The book highlights the current state of consciousness and the reasons behind the pain and agony many experience in relationships. The book lays down a new or alternative spiritual revolutionary foundation for relationships through awakening. The sole purpose of the book is to implore individuals to seek first the kingdom of God/Christ/Creator/All That Is which is within each individual living on earth.

It is within where the answers for many questions, true happiness, unconditional divine love awaits to be activated and it is at this space where forgiveness of self and others must be directed in order to find peace. This books also seeks to highlight the importance of karma and its role in our relationships and how when this concept of karma if understood a lot of pain and misery can be avoided.

The book seeks to point humanity to rise to higher consciousness through awakening. It is through awakening that God Realization and clarity shall be achieved. It is within the higher consciousness that true healing is realised as humanity will now perceive things as God/Christ/Buddha/All That Is perceives and a state of victory over self is achieved.

The book also emphasizes the concept of reincarnation and how if this concept is also acknowledged and understood, much more weight will be lifted from the agony suffered by individuals. And the fact that if reincarnation is understood then people can know that each soul that is incarnated here on planet earth, has been here before, possibly may be with the very spouse they live with and how soul contracts were signed before the current incarnation, as a result of the past pain each has caused the other and now because the roles have been exchanged the other must suffer the same in order to balance their karma.

The book summarises the origin of man, being in Oneness with God/ Christ/ Buddha/Creator/ All That Is, and how man's own creation of negative ego has separated man from God/Christ/Buddha/Creator/All That Is, which was demonstrated at the garden of Eden yet not truthfully depicted in the Bible.

The book seeks to encourage and spark a conversation, whereby when more questions in order to find the real truth, the old paradigm of control by the negative ego, the control and limitations by religion will collapse so that the ancient and original purpose can be re-established. And it is here where the walls of illusion when collapsed, each individual will be able to transcend this pain and find healing. It is here where individuals will realise the depth of negative ego's illusion that is not the true reality if transcended the reality of Truth of Oneness with God/Christ/Holy/Buddha/All That Is.

The book seeks to encourage people to self-mastery. Mastering of thoughts, feelings and actions that have created the reality we live in now and how if thought forms are mastered and aligned with Oneness with God objectivity can be applied, misunderstanding avoided resulting in healing and transformation of relationships from the individual level right until a family, community and/or a nation can be healed.

The book encourages readers to learn to differentiate between real truth and illusion, and how illusion has been created by the Negative Ego and how to transcend this negative ego and taking your power back from this negative ego that has so much influence in our subconscious mind. And the application of God Sovereign Truth and Christ Consciousness.

ACKNOWLEGEMENTS

Divine I AM Presence, I love Thee, I bless Thee, and I thank Thee for all Thy Love and outpouring of Divine energy. I bless the Holy Spirit (Maha Chohan) and the Ascended Masters for their love, dedication, selflessness and outpouring of light, their service and faith in me. I bless the Angelic Kingdom, Seraphim, Cherubim Kingdom, The Elohim of Creation, the Elementals and the Cosmic Devas and All Holy Heavenly beings for their service to me and all mankind. Blessings, knowledge, wisdom, courage, faith, power, purity, peace, Divine love, protection and all of God's Divine virtues, greatness and purpose.

I would like to thank my family for directly and indirectly supporting the work of this book. My husband for being part of the cast and playing his role so well. My kids, you guys are very special and I thank you for being the best co-workers I could ever have. Helping me and correcting me as and when it was needed and your unconditional love, I declare continuous blessings over your lives.

So much love and adoration goes to my extended family. I would like you to know that we each have a unique path to journey on and your understanding or the lack thereof is much appreciated. That is what diversity is all about; yet in Oneness in Christ.

How can I forget the special sisters in my life? Wow what a bunch of soul family you are. I love you and I am truly thankful for all the support you have given me. You have corrected me, reprimanded me, listened to me and some even took part in this path of awakening.

To everyone that has contributed to the drama of my life in order to give birth to this book, helping me to grow spiritually as you played your part either negatively or positively, I really do appreciate and love you so much and I speak blessings over your lives.

I would like to thank the Publisher: Inspired Publishing, you guys rock and I thank you so much for giving meaning to this book and packaging it the way I requested. Your patience as I gave you the run around every time is out of this world. Continue to grow and make the very best of self- publishers out there.

Finally, to the readers of this book: Wow! Thank you for giving me the opportunity to express myself through this book by lending me your ears and eyes so we can journey together on this exciting path.

With much Love .

Preface

Understanding the concept of consciousness and the state of human consciousness will help humanity to broaden its perspective on what has been set before people's eyes looking like challenges, attacks, and opposing energies especially in relationships.

This book seeks to highlight the extent of illusion and Ego that has separated the soul from the Creator. It will make you realise that what we see is a lie that we need to expose to allow healing and reawakening to the truth that will set many free.

This writing is based on a conversation I had with my I AM Presence during one of my early morning walks. The night before our conversation, I had pledged to serve and share the truths I had discovered. I had also promised to take action by sharing the truth about God's purpose with others, to expose the walls of illusion that have moulded us and need to be broken down.

While waiting for the Almighty to equip me with the energy to carry out this mission, I started decreeing love over every household I passed, street after street, and person after person as the spirit showed me their faces. When I did this, I was not just saying the words "I love", "I give love"; I had to pour out feelings of love and visualise Divine love covering each person, household, and area that the energy of love was being poured into. And right on my last lap, the voice of I AM Presence released into my heart "MARRIAGE REPACKAGED"!

With excitement and gratitude, I received the message and waited for more. The voice said, "Write a book about this topic, using your marriage experiences, the illumination and divine truths received concerning the original purpose of marriage and how each person should understand their purpose and align it with the divine purpose of God."

Your story of suffering and healing may help someone to overcome their suffering. Your joy and happiness may inspire others. Your ability to heal yourself may help someone else to understand themselves. Let your soul shine, and be the light to others like you, so you can find one another. Be the magnet and lighthouse for those who are lost. If you need help or are lost, ask that your light finds and connects with the lighthouse of God.

I have written this book with so much love, a selfless heart, and respect for others' opinions and beliefs. Dear reader, I request you to read it with an open mind and heart, it has the potential to revolutionarise your consciousness and change your life forever. May it serve as a mirror of your journey.

There are many unhappy people who feel that God has failed them. I hope this book will help them understand the mastering of self and see the God within each person. It will make people understand the spiritual aspects of relationships and recognise their true purpose, and that living in a physical body in this planet earth can be a wonderful thing.

In addition, it will help you break the walls of illusion to liberate Self by taking back power from Negative Ego, and allowing healing by opening your heart and mind to the energies of this book. Each chapter unlocks doors of liberation by allowing a different perspective to life.

The book is not meant to be read with a dense mind. Note that some or most of my experiences were part of my awakening or formed bridges to my awakening to self-mastery of thoughts, actions, emotions and taking back my power.

Throughout these experiences, I was more reactive to life. I was operating from the subconscious mind controlled by negative Ego; I gave my power to Ego to control things hence the messy outcome, however it has been an interesting journey. Now this book serves to enlighten those who are in the same path to awaken to the truth and take back their power from Ego and allow the Monad or the Superconscious or the Spirit to take over and guide them in Oneness with God Self.

CHAPTER ONE

THE STATE OF CONSCIOUSNESS

Every person in the universe operates in a certain state of consciousness and it can be a dense or a harmonised heavenly state. How we act, react to circumstances, treat others and view ourselves, be it self-hate or self- love, is determined by our state of consciousness.

Our state of consciousness determines how we judge others and ourselves, condemn, deal with guilt, and fail to allow healing to come forth. Changing our circumstances, freeing or healing ourselves, solely depends on the individual.

Those who have taken a step to awaken and move from the dense or polarised state of consciousness or third dimension state to a harmonised or heaven-on-earth state of consciousness are better off. However, it hurts to watch, daily, those who have remained in duality continue to drown in self-hatred, anger, guilt, arrogance, being judgemental, trapped in illusion, and projecting these energies onto others while refusing to get help. While wallowing in their deception, they go into every manner of escapism to ease their discord.

It pains me to see loved ones persist in their hardness of heart because of free will. These people can barely gasp for air filled with Divine Love.

I wrote this chapter on the morning when I received a scripture from I AM: "Behold we call them blessed who endured. You have heard of the perseverance of Job, and have seen the Lord in the outcome, and how the Lord is full of compassion and mercy." (James 5 vs11). Little did I know then how angry, heartbroken, and anxious I would be that day until late afternoon.

I shared my misery with a close friend. During our conversation I remembered that according to the Karmic Law, 21 Essential Lessons (a language many may not understand), a student applies for embodiment. He or she applies to transmute the extra-ordinate Karma caused in previous past lives. Later, in embodiment, the individual does not remember this request. When the person faces difficulties, he or she blames the Karmic board for the problems and wishes he or she was denied embodiment. The statement made me understand what was happening, and it gave me peace that took me back to my senses. I immediately felt healing covering my entire being.

I believe many of us have started marital relationships, with no expectation but just a dream of a perfect life, only to be disappointed.

The purpose of writing this book is to reach out to many that have been living under the illusions brought to all of us by negative forces, and our participation in the drama.

When I got married the first time, I did not understand it or have any intention of doing it. I decided to get married to the man because we had a child together; I did not even know anything about marriage or the person I was getting married to. Predictably, it did not work.

The purpose of writing this book is to reach out to many that have been living under the illusions brought to all of us by dark forces, and our participation in the drama.

When I got married for the second time, I was desperate to close that space and I do not know if I was getting married because I needed financial help. Does this sound familiar? I know that many men and women in relationships have plunged into marriages for the wrong reasons. Some get married because they love their partners and I must confess, in my case I was also in love with the person or I thought I was. I believe many of us start relationships with expectations but devoid of knowledge.

I must emphasise that we all have to walk our journey in discovering ourselves and it involves experiencing what I have alluded to above. For you to know who you are, it is important to embrace these painful experiences. They will empower you break the shell so that your true self may emerge.

When I was going through my painful experiences, I never heard or knew the word "soulmate" or "twin-flames" or it never mattered in my life. I thought I had found the one or I would make one out of what I had. This is an illusion that many young and old brothers and sisters have about each other and when they fail, they blame it on someone or God. It is time to stop behaving like a victim of circumstances and understand that you are responsible for what happens to your personal energy.

As much as I want to share my personal journey, which I believe mirrors so many people's experiences, it is important to note that you are not a victim and nobody has done you any wrong. Stop blaming other people or your "horrible childhood". By so doing, you are sending a message to the Universe that this is what you are; this is what you want; you are comfortable with it; and "please send me more".

Marrying for the wrong reasons and lack of commitment are major contributors to high rates of divorce. It does not matter how you look at it. "I fell out of love", "I no longer like the person", "I met someone new", "we have reached a point-of-no-return stage so we need to part ways," "she is not what I thought she is". People who are on the verge of separation or divorce utter these statements and these utterances are probably the reasons for separation, marital problems, cheating, oppression, aggression, isolation, and rejection.

These people would have started such relationships for the wrong reasons and they are bound to fail because Mighty I AM is not the foundation. Being separate from God, the Creator, the Source, is the reason we are divided into "them and us". It leads to failure to resolve our differences and understand the concept of marriage from the original plan.

You do not solve problems by either walking away or running away from them. Unless you face your monsters, you will never overcome them. For you to figure out how to face your challenges, you need to detach yourself from the relationship while you are still in it (I will dwell on this later in the book). You also need to consult with your inner self to understand your role in the whole drama. You may realise that you are the author of what you are experiencing and the next person is just playing their part of what you wrote or projected to them.

When you are emotional, it is difficult for you to be factual and face reality. In addition, you cannot hear the voice of the Holy Spirit unless you calm down; emotions cloud your judgement like intoxication. While I was hurting, I did not accept the fact that a human being created the challenges I faced, and not the environment. This person was just performing his role based on the script my soul had written and signed to manifest in my current life in order for me to awaken.

Many people think a change of environment changes a person or may help them start afresh. This mindset does not last, because they soon realise that the environment plays an insignificant role in changing a person. The decision to change rests on the preparedness of a person to transform.

You often have expectations regarding where you want to go, where you want your path to lead to, but is this the best thing for you to do?

What is the basis of these expectations? Is it experience? Or you are just following hearsay?

Great writers before me taught me that each person on earth has been here before. Before we reincarnate, we sign contracts with each other and karma has its role in how our lives are shaped. The Lord maintains and knows that in order for His students to awaken from their common indifference, they need to be shaken out of their comfort. When this happens, they are awakened from the state of fear and what Jesus called the "consciousness of death", where they always doubt whether the light will win over darkness, or whether calamity will befall them.

Let us explore the topic of suffering or unhappiness in relationships, especially marital ones. Many religious sects, especially Christianity, do not believe in this concept. However, this is a reality and the truth whether or not you believe it. Past life and reincarnation, or re-embodiment or enlightenment or rebirth, is a reality that will provide answers to the current questions if we follow and understand it.

We have lived other lives before this current one and we signed contracts in those lifetimes. Those contracts govern, to a certain degree, the lives we live. We are living in the momentum of energy that allows us to remember who we truly are, but you need a reminder. The reminder may come as suffering to trigger you to remember or reawaken your ancient memories. To understand these memories, you must heal your soul.

Triggers to offset suffering are negotiated among souls before birth. These are known as "soul contracts". You would find that the person you are married to now was your partner in the previous lifetime, and you experienced pain, suffering, passion, attraction, and unhappiness then. Sometimes, you find that you were not healed. Now, in the current lifetime, because of amnesia during rebirth, the two of you cannot remember these experiences.

For example, you would find that a couple has had a soul contract for their current lifetime, each agreed to embody the energy of wholeness and unconditional love to become the frequency holders for others, not as a couple, but as separate individuals to show others that you do not have to live a life in limited misery.

It is normal to fall in love, learn from it, grow from it, and fall out of it. You are not bound to one person forever just because you felt passion which later turned into jealousy, and a need to control one another. A couple in that situation needs to recreate its experiences so that both individuals could remember their ancient soul memories that will serve them and others in their mission.

Many have memories of pain, unhappiness, suffering, passion, attraction, and happiness in their past lifetimes, but because there was no soul healing, and the karma accumulated, they need to come back and relive these experiences. However, the roles have now been swapped. As a couple, one of you has caused the other so much pain and sorrow resulting in accumulated karma. Now, in this lifetime, you remarry the same person either as a male or female depending on your soul contract and you need to suffer the same pain you caused the other in the past lifetime.

Each person must allow healing and this will also depend on whether the suffering has triggered awakening that will seek the help of higher beings, our soul family, our higher selves, or our Creator, to set this in motion. Seeking the truth will help you to see the original pain in your soul. Without soul healing, this experience will be relived lifetime after lifetime as long as the ancient memories are not triggered for the healing process to take place.

We should also keep in mind that change takes time. There will be no change until you are ready to see everything as it is. You must realise that you are the creator of your misery, and you are the only one who can change it. You are not the victim you believe you are; but you are disconnected from your higher self and God.

No amount of deliverance (practiced by Christian and other religions) can completely heal a soul and its past life pain and suffering. Each person must take this journey to heal themselves and change their perspective from being a victim to realising that we are the authors of our own life drama.

We all get used to our routines as a function of survival circuit, and its only until something cracks the glass or we are pushed so hard that we notice that the world has become so small and it is time to make changes. It all starts within; answers lie within you.

CHAPTER TWO

THE ENEMY WITHIN AND AMONG US

While you are hurting, be careful of people you allow into your space and the impact they make. Many people may sound sympathetic when they are not and that is not helpful in your journey to overcome pain, humiliation, rejection, and loss. You need people that will help you face the monster without losing yourself to hatred and unforgiveness. You need people that believe in you, people who have walked that path, and this comes from people you least expect.

At one time, I was hurting and beyond myself. I confined myself to isolation. I was so ashamed after one huge, embarrassing moment when my car and all my clothes were taken and given to a girlfriend or should I call her "a sidekick". After court orders and making a fool of myself, by physically attacking the sidekick at a restaurant, I received an unusual visit from a sister. She was not a friend or someone close to me. Initially, I did not want to entertain her when she came to my house. I even refused to open the door for her by playing absent.

The sister persisted and told me that she would not leave until I opened the door and guess what! Her words, wisdom, and support encouraged me. She brought me out of my dungeon and told me how ok it was for me to feel the way I did. She assured me that I was not alone, the entire town was behind me, and many people looked up to me. The sad thing is that the perpetrators always walk tall and see nothing wrong with their actions.

Writing this book has brought many painful memories. We normally tell ourselves that we are healed or are fine until we face a similar challenge or its memory.

The saying: "A wound only heals once it is out in the open", applied to me and I realised how true it is. I thought I was over my experiences and that I was healed, but I discovered that I had only covered my pain. I did not realise that my decision not to deal with it did not mean that it was not there.

I did not know how broken I was until the deep memories of pain, each with its own experiences, unravelled. I can imagine how women who have gone through what I have experienced handle their pain. I also sympathise with those who are going through it now.

I am not sharing the details of my journey to entice you with gossip, but to highlight the fact that everything; every single step I took, and what happened to me resulted from my soul contract. You may call it a pattern, yes I will agree with you, because it becomes a pattern when you want to fight it, reason it out, resist it, or pray it away. Unless you face that pattern, allow it to flow through, accept it, forgive those involved and yourself, It will continue to recur. You need to learn from it, grow from it, and let go of pain.

Therapists advise some people to walk away while it is still early and some do so. Some, unfortunately, lose their lives to either diseases caused by this pain or the abuse itself.

Suffering in the hands of a broken abuser is a topic for another book. However, it is more difficult for a person to suffer continually yet in different ways in the hands of the same perpetrator. When do you get time to forget if you stay in a relationship and endure the suffering?

However, the soul contract that resulted in us volunteering to be subjected to a bombardment of thought forms, emotions and energies that will test each volunteer to the core, is playing a bigger role we need to accept.

Gabriel Raio Lunar asserts that these tests have been divided into phases. In the first phase, situations that a volunteer will face are presented, intensively, related to their soul program. It shows how they will behave, and what their potential reactions to challenges will be. For each reaction presented by the being in the face of its vicissitudes, a "score" which is directly linked to what would be "ideal" for its mission, is automatically generated and will be accounted for at the end of other phases.

After the completion of the first phase in the "simulator", the being will be exposed to the second. In this phase, all beings and energies that will be "against" the individual during their mission will be presented to them. The individual will be shown the intense spiritual persecutions to which they will be subjected, and the energies that will try to drag them from their mission. The individual will also be shown the intentions and actions of innumerable beings, incarnated and disincarnated, that work to ensure complete failure of their mission. Just as in the first phase, a score is generated in line with the reactions that a being expresses.

In the third phase, the being is exposed to an intense "romantic" relationship and a strong affectionate connection.

We normally tell ourselves that we are healed or are fine until we face a similar challenge or its memory.

However, at the time of his or her mission, this romantic connection will be the "dividing line" between following their mission or romantic path depending on the choice each of them make. It is necessary in the detachment of that context to be able to jump to another line where the mission is to be continued.

This is where you are called to a certain mission in the fabric of life to impact lives greatly, however, there is opposition from your partner who does not agree with your mission and wants you to choose between them and the mission. This can be a career or business move. The conflict leads to bifurcation from the partner and in this instance many choose to stay.

In most cases, the detachment from what tries to limit him or her, is the sufficient impulse for the being to meet those loving souls who have great energetic affinity or who have great kinship of soul. Encounters of similar souls, twins, is the crucial point to remain in the old energy to which you are familiar or to move on, unified to your real love and thus to continue your mission of anchoring the new consciousness in the environment where you are. It is clear that a constellation of challenges will rise in this important decision. From the reactions to these questions, a "score" is also generated.

At the end of the three phases, the "scores" are counted and the sum can have a total of a maximum of 100 and a minimum of 99.5 for the master to pass the Holographic Reality Simulator Test. If the missionary passes the three tests, there will be another one with intensity doubled. Everything that the missionary experienced and challenged in the first test will be intensified doubly to ensure that there is real capacity to deal with that situation. An example of one missionary who incarnated on earth and passed the test is King Solomon.

It is necessary to note that even if the missionary passes the simulator test, there is no guarantee that they will execute their mission with inviolable mastery. Many who have passed through the simulator, descended, and got lost in the pain of reality. No matter how much the holographic simulator is needed, nothing compares to direct immersion in reality. The intention here is to make us understand our challenges, how to play our part in dancing in polarity, and stop holding unnecessary grudges. We just dance along, absorb, accept, forgive, and let go and use each experience as a stepping-stone.

The experiences I am sharing with you led to this truth, the I AM truth regarding marriage, the Divine purpose of marriage and noting that this is a path of self-love, Divine love, the original love of our Father Mother God. The sooner you realise that everything is an illusion and that the longer you hang on to it, the longer it will take for you in the evolution of life. In every situation, the sooner you make the choice to let go, the better. The more you hold on to things, perceptions, belief systems, and old ways of doing things, the harder it will become to accept change. We are victims of our own actions and the sooner we accept this, the better.

Love is the language of life that we need to learn. We have to learn its truth and origin and being in Oneness with Love (God). Failure to accept this truth will result in us living in a tunnel of separation within ourselves, from God, and His very creation. This separation has led Ego to decide how you view those around you. It also makes you see them as separate beings from you.

Love is the very fabric of Creation. It can be vast, fiery, and soft. It can be tough and scour all that is not yours away from within your being like a desert wind. Love can fill your heart until it overflows with an expansive ache (The Council of Nine Eliza Ayres). https://www.thestarseedhighway.com

We were led to where we are today; however, we must consider that we fully participated. Hence, accepting and understanding the concept of incarnation, past lives and our origin will assist us in our personal journeys.

You have to accept that situations you found yourself in and people that came into your life, in different forms, to "hurt" you, were contracted by you. What you project through thoughts and feelings are the energies of how you view yourself in separation and self-hate, doubt, and fear. These projections are picked up by the universe as an invite from you saying: "Send me more please", and the universe is not biased; it will give you exactly what you asked for.

I learned that fighting back, in whatever way does not bring victory as many people think. The word "fight" in my understanding should never have been in the vocabulary in the first place. For whom are you fighting? What are you fighting? Who is this that you even want God to get involved in your battle? You are the enemy. Stop pointing fingers at others, go within, and help yourself by forgiving and letting go to set yourself on a path of self-discovery, self-awareness and Oneness with God-Christ Consciousness.

CHAPTER THREE

VIOLENCE IN A RELATIONSHIP

Many of us battling with what has been imposed on us by the powers that were, illusion, hatred, fear, anger and separation, resulting in the violence we find ourselves exposed to, are both victims and perpetrators of our own circumstances, however I will elaborate much on this topic later in the book.

It is important for you to search deeper for the causes of challenges you face. As my journey in search for the truth continued, I discovered that I was meant to walk through this path of pain. My soul signed a contract with the soul of my loved one to be where we were. What I have mentioned above did not happen by chance; it was my choice; my contract; and my karma.

If we all can learn more about the concept of Karma and Incarnation, we can avoid a lot of pain and misery. As we went through our challenges, there was no memory about the contract we signed before we reincarnated in this lifetime. I know I may sound controversial, but my search for the truth has landed me on this path of truth, the path of forgiveness, the path of compassion, the path of unconditional love, the path of awakening, and I am truly grateful for this truth.

Many people, especially women, have been physically abused in so many ways over a long period, but it is good not to dwell in the past. Ladies, you cannot expect a person who does not love himself or does not know what love is to give you what he does not have. Buying gifts, expensive clothes, cars, bags, food, and going on expensive holidays is not love; having meaningless sex is not love. It is delusional for you to expect a person who does not know who he is to understand you.

Many people mistake lust for love and fall into it only to awaken days, months, or years later wondering who the person they are married to is. We can take this as a lesson and move on. I had many opportunities to walk away, but something in me told me that I am not a coward. Walking away is not a solution for you, because you will carry your wounds with you wherever you will go and, it opens a door of divorce curses for your descendants. I told myself that if I could not fix the person, at least I could make them pay for the pain they had caused me. That cannot happen if you walk away. I stayed true to my purpose no matter how difficult it was.

Please do not get me wrong, my intention here is not to badmouth or to expose anyone, but to demonstrate what illusion, separateness, anger, bitterness, rejection, and self-hate do to people. My intention is to help those who may be going through some of the experiences I went through to overcome their own.

The pain imposed by a broken child cuts deep. The bullies you see are victims of bullying themselves. I discovered that we are both victims and perpetrators of our own circumstances.

Violence of whatever nature is wrong and cannot be condoned. However, our lack of knowledge can cause pain. I have read quite several books about marriage and relationships, but failed to get the peace and answers I needed or expected. Please do not get me wrong, my intention is not to criticise other authors, but to encourage a deep search for the meaning of life. I searched for the root of my problems on both my partner's side and my side of the pie. And I need to mention that I was not only the victim here, but the perpetrator too.

It is easy to point fingers at others without taking responsibility for your part in the demise of a union. I also have my broken past. My father rejected me when my mother was pregnant and the rejection forced her to attempt suicide. A single mother raised me but she died of cancer while I was young.

As a young person, I was surrounded by an angry family: my grandmother, aunts, uncles, and cousins. We grew up being called names, and there was a lot of anger, hatred, resentment, jealousy, and all sorts of negativity around. The unfortunate part is that I never had an opportunity to ask those who have now departed about the source of their anger.

While awakening, I am trying very hard to bring this awareness to my relations to help them ease their anger, pain, unforgiveness, and separateness.

Looking back now, I somehow contributed to the toxic environment- the anger, aggression, and resentment. I became very reserved and moody. I could not maintain relationships or friendships, because I did not know how to. I had this element of aggression that always clouded my judgment in many things. I was angry, although I was not sure why I was. However, later in life, to be exact, as I was writing this book and also seeking answers, my higher self, my guides, informed me that the aggression and rage I had was a result of our DNA strands being ripped from us by team dark eons of time ago. In addition, I had never allowed myself to heal from this experience; I carried it lifetime after lifetime. However, I am grateful that I have now received my healing and I am still healing even now.

When I look at those around me now, especially my relatives who are still alive, I see so much animosity, so much anger, and pain. The sad thing is that this is being passed down to younger generations. I must mention that yes, we grew up in warmth and laughter, but when we spoke our tongues were filled with anger most of the time. I am still battling with this right now.

We grew up being intimidated and coerced to do things. I see myself doing this to my own kids and in the process, breaking them further. By threatening them all the time, I realise I am losing them.

While awakening, I am trying very hard to bring this awareness to my relations to help them ease their anger, pain, unforgiveness, and separateness. I believe that when you choose a path and step into a path of transition, help reaches you.

CHAPTER FOUR

HEALING ONESELF

During my meditations that morning while I was writing this chapter, my attention was drawn to this verse in the book of Galatians: "But the fruit of the Spirit is love, joy, peace (character as an inward state), long-suffering, gentleness, goodness (character in expression towards men), faith, meekness, temperance (character in expression towards God)" (Galatians 5vs22).

Christ's character is not mere moral and legal correctness, but the possession and manifestations of nine graces. When I read the scripture, I realised my shortcomings. I saw myself naked before God's presence as I was exposed to myself through the lenses of His Word.

How do I judge others about their morality, yet my character is in tatters? How do I see other people's faults while my expression towards others is 0% rated in terms of God's principles of love? How can I win or direct others to Christ while I lack faith in others attaining perfection and do not display meekness? How do I direct others when I am arrogant and temperamental?

Truly, this path is two-way and we should not be biased. We need balance, and we can only attain this through constant introspection and changing towards Christ consciousness. My attention is drawn to this principle: The power of silence; the need of the sincere student to become still more often throughout the course of the day. This allows the energy, directives, radiation, and power of God's presence to flow into the four lower vehicles and the outer consciousness and nourish them.

During these still moments, one receives a unique perspective of life and experiences the actions of others. In these still moments, the voice of the Holy Spirit or your guides will gently point you to the bigger picture that includes eternal healing and forgiveness.

I tried many self-help therapies available before I found this peace. I tried different prayer patterns and went for several deliverance sessions, yet nothing changed. I pleaded the blood of Jesus, violent prayers, casting out evil spirits, supplication prayers, thanksgiving prayers, and a lot of remedies out there. They only worked for a little while or did not work at all sometimes. The reason here is not because prayer does not help but how we have been taught to go about it.

It took me decades of anger, pain, and misery to get here. I remember one particular Friday in July; I was furious with God. I remember the horrible words I said about Him for His failure to come through for me. I considered Him non-existent. I told Him I was disappointed because he had failed me after I had served Him, obeyed His commands, and was faithful to the "useless" marriage. Wow, what a drama queen I had become! Pain can turn a person into an ungrateful monster.

So on this day, I ranted like most days when I was at my lowest low. I felt the unfairness of life on me. I went to sleep in my anger, and nothing happened until the following morning. I woke up with a heavy heart, yet I went on with my daily routines.

At around 11:00a.m the following morning while I was sweeping the passage, a gentle voice spoke to me. It was such a calming voice; I looked around and did not see anyone. The voice continued and assured me:

"I have heard your prayer and I have forgiven you. I am releasing a job for you, I am taking you to a higher level and favour, your children are mine already, and you must pray for the first born. Your husband is also mine." You should have seen me, I asked for forgiveness for my insults and God said, "I did not hear them, I only heard the cry of a desperate child." Right there He warned me about the company I kept.

You see this could have happened the night before during my ranting but it did not. God cannot enter a space full of anger and hatred. We spend most of our quiet time harbouring thoughts of negativity, anger, resentment, judgement, and this blocks our process of healing. Many times, we pray so much or make so much noise thinking we are talking to God but our hearts are not in the right place. When you are miserable, you can only entertain thoughts of misery. However, have we ever considered a different strategy to get our message across?

Has it ever occurred to you that the situations you find yourself in are there to teach you something and therefore you need to remain calm?

From that day, a lot changed in my life; not that my circumstances changed, but I changed for the greater. I had many conversations with God like never before. I was directed to some of the greatest philosophies of life that have transformed me into who I am today; many questions I had asked before were answered. I was directed to books I never thought I would read. The truth I held was turned upside down.

I had to unlearn many lies that had shaped my present to take in the truth, the truth that has set me free. For the first time in many years, I experienced real freedom; genuine happiness that I had been longing for landed at my doorstep and I welcomed it with both arms. I threw logic and Ego out of the window so I could receive the truth that has gradually healed my wounds, one phase at a time, and I am grateful.

The healing process does not have to focus only on one aspect of life or challenges you have faced, but it needs to be broad. Because there is a lot at stake in relationships, I will break down all the steps to be considered during the healing process. These steps are based on my own experiences. Take for instance, the concept of love; many people have misunderstood it. Has our understanding of love or how it has been brought happiness or satisfaction in relationships? I will, however, leave this to prominent scholars, academics, and experts.

During my research to find solutions to my problems, I read many books and each one made me search for more truth, as what I read did not really resonate with me. In addition, the practices did not give me the remedy I expected. I borrowed the following from one great author Gary Zukav who wrote about the living flame of love:

"The mystic and Saint John of the Cross said the goal of life, our ultimate union with God, can only be achieved through this 'living flame of love'.

Because the heart centre and its love fires are so essential to our physical, emotional and spiritual vitality, the initiations and lessons that involve the heart are some of the most profound we will ever encounter."

In these still moments, the voice of the Holy Spirit or your guides will gently point you to the bigger picture that includes eternal healing and forgiveness.

We must understand that each individual's journey is unique. Therefore, your higher self, guides, and council are yours and assigned to you according to your Oneness with Christ. The messages you receive during your meditations are meant for you and your path. Each person is the saviour of his or her own path and must stop expecting others to come and save him or her.

We are all travellers individually and collectively to transform our planet earth and each must first save and master themselves to master the global challenges collectively. People have their own script and challenges in line with their soul contracts. People involved are players you picked to be part of your own drama in the symphony of life and the path of remembering who you are and clearing your karma.

You have a choice. You can change your existence; you have a right to a peaceful and joyful life. The universe is fully aware of your potential and now it is time to acknowledge it yourself. The power of change is within you and has always been yours.

While meditating I came across a blog about healing and it got my attention. As I read the experiences of the blogger who highlighted the effects of the exploitation of nature, I could see the damage that is happening globally. It reminded me about my jogging that morning and how I felt every time I passed a group of people. Each time I passed a group of about three or more, I sensed an energy surge out of me that left me drained. As a result, I could hardly breathe, or walk. This happened about three to four times in that seven-kilometre jog.

This experience reminded me about Jesus in Luke 8vs 43-46 where he Jesus was touched by the woman with the issue of blood. He asked who touched him because he felt part of His power leaving him. She touched Jesus, believing that she would get her healing, and this happened within a group of people who were pushing and pulling to get His attention. Many people touched Him, but there was something different about this woman's touch.

Because I am learning a lot about Jesus's path and experiences to apply them in my path, I am also learning how to help in healing the land in a small way that I can. And in this instance, where I was jogging, I intended to radiate or project the light of God and His Divine love wherever I passed. I am still learning and need more lessons about energy healing and protection; I opened myself up to some energy pulling from others, hence I was so drained every time I passed a group of people. I believe I felt drained, because each group pulled off my energy simultaneously.

Later, as I was trying to find answers to my physical condition after the jog, I remembered the responsibility we all have as individuals to collectively heal our mother earth. People have subjected the earth to so much destruction and exploitation and its desperation to cleanse itself results in the calamities we see globally. So while working on healing our souls, let us endeavour to help heal our land in any way we can to restore harmony with mother earth. Beloved we can do better and stop focusing on things that really do not matter.

The most important thing is that in the plane of Consciousness we live in and the other side, man has free will. Each individual through his or her thoughts, feelings, and actions sets up courses for the future. A person is the creator of his or her own future irrespective of religious affiliation, race, or colour.

In physical embodiment, it appears we are separate from God; this is not true. God is closer than our breath. Regardless of what the evidence may show, we as individuals in physical embodiment are still connected to our I Am Presence, which is anchored in our hearts. The Son (I AM Presence) has not and will never lose His connection to the Father (Helios and Vesta) and the Holy Spirit (Alpha And Omega), the supplier of life energy for our galaxy.

Before the fall of man, there was visual contact with God's helpers, the Ascended Host. We must look within the inner eye, become still, and follow within. Our I AM Presence, our connection to God is our ever-present help in times of distress, during illness and times of financial lack.

In addition, we can call on the help of the Ascended Host. This is our God-given privilege. Therefore, physical embodiments should not prevent us from demonstrating perfection. Actually, they have given us an opportunity to do so. Any experience should be viewed with the lens of the inner eye looking beyond the testimony of the five senses.

We must acknowledge that God is not the dispenser of sin, sickness, and death, but the giver of every perfect gift. We must know that imperfect conditions occur only through incorrect use of energy by the individual. Each person can contribute towards reversing the situation through proper and constructive use of energy.

This energy may be used in healing the sick if the individual or student calls upon the Mighty I AM Presence into action, making it the only authority over the discordant condition. Physicians need to understand that the physical body is only one of the seven bodies and humanity must understand that we need the medical profession in today's conditions. A cordial relationship between the physicians and spiritual healers is necessary.

However, while we need spiritual help, the list below gives access to the Divine infinite perfection of God's 12 Aspects or Virtues that will help in our daily needs. The Twelve Solar Aspects of Deity are:

PROTECTION: Archangel Michael and Lady Faith, Ascended Master El Morya, Elohim Hercules are there to ensure the Will of God, illumined faith, power and protection. God's first cause of perfection is just a call away.

WISDOM: We call on Archangel Jophiel and Christine, Ascended Masters, Lanto, Kuthumi, Elohim Apollo, and Lumina. They are the God Virtue of wisdom, illumination, Christ consciousness, enlightenment, understanding, perception, and constancy.

DIVINE LOVE: The Divine love of God is the need of all mankind and God's Virtue of transfiguring Divine love, adoration, tolerance and Oneness. Reference of all life is represented by Archangel Chamuel and Charity, Ascended Master Paul the Venetian, Maha Chohan, Lady Rowena, Lady Nada, Mighty Victory and Elohim Heros and Amora.

PURITY AND RESTORATION: Calling for help for the clearing of energy debris to establish purity and restoration. Archangel Gabriel and Hope, Ascended Master Serapis Bay, Elohim Astrea and Clair will remove the courses and cores of the discordant condition. In addition, one can visualise the healing presence of one of the above Masters.

HEALING: We call on the Ascended Master who specialises in healing and mercy (Mother Mary, Archangel Raphael, Lord Jesus, Lady Nada, Hillarion (Apostle Paul), Kwan Yin (the Goddess of Mercy and Compassion). The said beings represent the God's virtue or aspect of illumined truth, healing, consecration, and inner vision.

DIVINE PEACE: Beloved Lord Jesus and Lady Nada, Archangels Uriel and Aurora, Elohim Peace and Aloha and Ascended Master John the Beloved, the representatives of God's Divine grace, peace, healing, devotional worship and the manifestation of Christ.

TRANSMUTATION: This is followed by calling on the Law of Forgiveness and the Violet Transmuting Flame (Ascended Master Saint Germain, Archangel Zadkiel and Lady Amethyst and Elohim Acturus) to ensure God's infinite perfection, mercy, compassion, forgiveness, transmutation, liberty, justice, freedom and victory.

CLARITY: Archangels Aquariel and Lady Clarity, Lord Larveen, Elohim Bromwell and Joyce are the Divine representatives of God's qualities of clarity, Divine perception, and discernment.

HARMONY AND BALANCE: God's infinite perfection of balance and harmony is brought forth by Archangels Anthriel and Harmony, Lady Prizma and Lord Yananda, Lady Minerva and goddess of harmony and Elohim Manetta and Golda. In them, one calls for harmony, balance, assurance, and God's confidence.

PROSPERITY: If it is a financial need that needs to be addressed, Lord Krishna, Archangel Valories and Lady Peace, Lady Isis and Elohim Claudine, goddess of change and Angels of abundance are

God's virtue of eternal peace, prosperity, abundance, and God's supply of all good things.

DIVINE PURPOSE: For Divine purpose, enthusiasm, and joy, we call for God's Virtues Archangel Anthriel, Lady Harmony, Lord Genitus, Lady Rosemary, Elohim Theos and Lady Crispa.

TRANSFORMATION AND TRANSFIGURATION: We call on

Archangels Jychondria and Lady Opalescence, Lady Wonderous and Lord Owin and Elohim Emos and Lady Unifa.

The above newly anchored Violet Flame of God's Infinite Perfection is so powerful that it pulsates with the perfect balance of our Father God's fifth Dimensional Crystalline Solar Frequency of the Masculine Blue Flame of Divine Power and our Mother God's fifth Dimensional Crystalline solar Frequencies of the Feminine Pink Flame of Divine Love.

When the Masculine and Feminine Polarities of our Father-Mother God's Crystalline Light merge into a perfectly balanced Violet Flame, everything this Sacred Fire embraces is lifted to a higher expression of its Divine potential and infinite perfection than it was previously able to express.

The New Violet Flame of God's Infinite Perfection pulsates with all of the Divine qualities we have known and associated with the Violet Flame: forgiveness, mercy, compassion, transmutation, Divine ceremony, justice, liberty, freedom, and victory. Now the full Divine momentum of God's infinite perfection permeates every aspect of this Sacred Fire as well.

The Cosmic Being of Light known as Saint Germain is still the keeper of the Violet Flame for this Universe. He has evolved into a higher expression of his Divine self in order to expand this New Crystalline Solar Violet Flame in, through, and around every facet of life on Earth during the 2,000-plus years that we will be held in the embrace of the Age of Aquarius.

This is not wishful thinking. As we come closer to God, the rate of vibration of our physical body will be accelerated and its beauty, purity, and perfection will once manifest and any negative energy cannot get any close.

CHAPTER FIVE

WAITING ON GOD

The illusions of power are shocking; they make people want to control others in relationships and in every aspect of life. Relationships or marriages are not about control or power, for if they were, many people would not be in the peeved positions they are in because they lost control over others.

Relationships should be rooted in love. Divine love has no jealousy or control, and it is not oppressive. When someone has a different view from yours, it does not mean that they are wrong, and you do not lose your power by accepting different views.

As I type this, I recall a week ago I had a phone call from a lady who desperately wanted to talk to me. I availed myself hoping that it was a call about a property or something similar. I was disappointed when I heard the reason for her call. It is so painful when people that you look up to go through challenges similar to yours.

We made an appointment to meet the next morning. When she arrived at the set venue, we discussed the issue she had raised the previous day. I was hurt to see her helpless; she was so desperate to hear the voice of hope. As I was trying to assure her and telling her not to worry and that everything was in God's hands, my other half arrived. We told him about the issue and surprisingly; he gave the lady hope and assured her that there was nothing to worry about; it was just paperwork, and maybe her husband's actions were for business purposes.

The point I want to raise is that the lady's concerns over the manner in which her husband had acted was like what I had been through more than once. Even at the time she approached me I was not sure where I stood except for I AM's assurance that nothing would happen to me. I was shocked by the manner in which my other half advised her; he spoke with so much wisdom, but the actions of the spouse were like his.

The bottom line is many people, if not all people in relationships, are broken in one way or the other and think going separate ways is the answer. Divorce does not heal your brokenness; it deepens it. A shattered soul cannot do anything beyond what it only knows- brokenness. It cannot help itself or other souls. A shattered soul thinks hurting another will make it feel better or heal, but there is no truth in this.

I used the example above to illustrate that all or most marriages go through turmoil resulting in divorce. My view is that the turmoil can be avoided if the following issues are addressed first:

a) What has drawn the two of you to each other? Is it needy love or unconditional love? Needy love can blind you.

b) Is the relationship based on needs for one another, need for energies (pieces of puzzles) they lacked?

c) Will the two live to meet each other on neutral ground and learn to compromise or is the relationship based on a give-and-take basis?

d) What were you missing when you first met your partner?

e) What triggers you?

f) What attracts you to the person and arouses passion for them. For this can be driven by the missing piece of the puzzle, something you subconsciously feel you want.

Eva Marquez, in Pleiadian Code: The Soul Rescue, says the passion and attraction one feels when finding that right person is just the energy of a missing piece of the puzzle; something you subconsciously feel you want or need.

She further states that next time you feel attracted to someone, just ask yourself what attracts you the most to this person? Maybe he or she is outspoken, and you are shy and wish to be a proficient speaker. Maybe the person has a beautiful body, and you admire that body. It could be anything. So, be honest with yourself before you fall in love; give yourself that which you are attracted to first.

For example, if you are shy then work on your confidence. Once you find it and the person still attracts you, then it could be genuine love that will last; not an attraction to something you subconsciously need or want.

Some experiences can be connected to culture, for example, in some communities if a woman cannot meet her daily needs, she looks for that person who will help pay the bills, and buy happiness. The foundation of such a relationship is flawed. Some financially stable women are not easily approachable by their male counterparts. Men perceive such women to be threats. If a relationship develops between a man and such a woman, it may be strained because of Ego or patriarchy. The man would feel that the supposed domination of the female takes his power away, and this flawed perception may lead to divorce or separation.

Many aspects that affect relationships must be looked at spiritually before applying the physical mind. Yes, I know I may not be a love expert but without God, a union is weak and hardly stands.

Do not confuse love for something you are missing. Ask yourself: what am I missing? What triggers me? Instead of trying to change someone, change yourself; identify your weaknesses and your blockages. Heal your soul, find unconditional love, and see how your change affects the other person. Go within yourself often, do not be afraid to open the door of dark and light and accept both sides as equal forces.

Naturally, you are afraid of darkness, but darkness is a natural part of you and accepting it will open the hidden door into the ultimate power you have and are afraid of. Like God, you can create or destroy with a simple thought; it depends on what you choose. The one who holds the power has integrity aligned to the higher self and God.

Transcending the duality into Oneness and fully embodying it within is the key to the ultimate soul power.

You cannot change someone to be what you want them to be, but accept them the way they are. Respect their choices and love them unconditionally. You should accept one another the way you are and surrender to the will of God.

If you meet your twin flame, find your missing pieces, change yourself, and see if your relationship develops to true unconditional love. Ask yourself if it is a happy-ever-after or just another opportunity to find what you needed for your soul healing. Life is too short; do not live it in heartbreaks, bitterness, anger, or sadness.

It is through awakening or enlightenment that you see challenges and suffering differently. You cease to look at them as black and white, good or bad, but see everything as just an experience, an opportunity for the soul and spirit to grow. This process will help you to look beyond any differences between you and others. It will also help you not focus on human judgements, but on unconditional love.

Focusing on negativity and problems is the work of the human Ego and this must change. You need to focus on changing your perception and shifting your focus from problems to changing and saving the world. You do that by overcoming your own Ego so you come into that Oneness with your own higher self and God.

Instead of running around, be at peace, a state of calm, which is the higher bliss of being. You may ask how you become peaceful when everything is falling apart and your marriage is not working, you are jobless, and cannot pay your bills. Remember the Bible verse, "Be still and know that I AM God." That is I AM saying, "Be at peace, focus on Oneness with me, I AM all that you need."

It is in the state of Oneness, calm, and peace that you will hear the voice of God. It is in this state of being that you ask for direction and wait for an answer. It is written in the book of Acts: "And being assembled together with them, He commanded them not to depart from Jerusalem, but wait for the promise of the Father which sayeth He, ye have heard of me...." (Acts 1:14). Jesus makes the promise here, but the condition for its fulfilment is waiting. Let us unpack what one must wait for.

One must wait for the Holy Spirit. Who is the Holy Spirit? It is the Divine inspiration of God, the creative force and aspect of God. There are many aspects of God the Creator, like the I AM aspect, the masculine and the feminine aspects of God, to name a few. Before I dwell much on the aspects of God, lets us learn more about the Holy Spirit and what you do while waiting.

I believe Jesus said more to His disciples but those parts might have been left out of this instruction. What do you do while waiting? What exactly should happen during this waiting? And many other questions that needed answers. Most people are not patient and many things can happen while they are waiting. As a result of this, they may lose their position.

I can imagine the overwhelming anxiety that the disciples felt while waiting for the promise to be fulfilled. There is a likelihood that there was doubt, and they were afraid that the Promise might not come at all. Some disciples might have questioned the ability of the Holy Spirit to solve some problems or asked questions such as, "What if the Holy Spirit is not good enough for me?" "What if Jesus miscalculated and I may not be included in the number to receive the outpouring?" "What if He comes in the colour or form I may dislike?" Many other questions may have discouraged them. However, the scriptures have not mentioned them, so I guess they just waited quietly until the grand arrival of the Holy Spirit.

Well, they waited in prayer; they meditated and worked on themselves. They learnt to master themselves by not allowing thoughts of doubt, fear, anxiety, and noisy voices to distract them from receiving the Holy Spirit. They did not allow their financial lack to distract them, or the sicknesses, offence, judgement, unforgiveness, and the density of polarity to stop them from receiving the Holy Spirit. They placed their focus on the Creator; they went into their sacred hearts and built relationships there with the Creator. They opened their minds and hearts to the unseen world of wonder.

When all this happened, their surroundings had not changed. Lack, hatred, judgment, sickness, offence, and many other aspects of polarity were still very much there. Maybe they had even intensified, but they learned to master the ability to move and look beyond that and focus on their relationship with the Creator. Each of them knew that this was a journey travelled individually, and no one would stand in the gap for another to receive what Christ had promised. Each one had to work on his or her own path, master it, and overcome.

In addition, during this waiting, I believe there was no time to judge others. There was no time to point fingers and magnify the surrounding problems. Their focus was only on receiving the Holy Spirit. There was no time to worry about what they would eat the following day, week, or month, and who would pay the bills while they were waiting. The focus had to be on 'being here and now'.

In order to elaborate on this topic I want us to look at the truth while we wait for the Holy Spirit or the Voice of God. I am going to borrow from a blog by Patricia Cota – Roble's Dictation explaining what exactly happened. Let me also explain that upon realising this truth, I went further to research and I stumbled on the writing or dictations by Mother Mary and Jesus himself through Mr Guy W Ballard from the Ascended Masters Teaching Foundation.

When someone has a different view from yours, it does not mean that they are wrong, and you do not lose your power by accepting different views.

THE TRUTH ABOUT THE PENTACOSTAL DAY

Guy Ballard asserts that this day actually signifies the truth about the purpose of the Crucifixion of Jesus and His Resurrection, which the powers that were misconstrued to keep humanity in the dark, not knowing that we are Sons and Daughters of God.

Jesus and Mary Magdalene came as Avatars during the Piscean Age as it was purposed. His Divine mission was not to save humanity from sin as it has been told to prevent humanity from awakening to the coming of Mother God.

His Divine mission was to awaken humanity to its divinity.

- To lead humanity to the path of Oneness and Divine love and awaken humanity to the attainment of the Christ consciousness.

- The number thirty-three is the master number representing Christ Made Manifest the Christ consciousness.

- He was aware of our Egos and lack of trust of ourselves. In addition, how we missed the truth given by the former Avatars.

- His mission was to dispel the misconception that we are all dirty sinners born of a sinful nature that needs a saviour and that He Jesus is that Saviour.

- No matter how much you loved Him and confirmed Him as your Lord and Saviour, He himself cannot save you. You must save yourself.

- The gift of free will does not allow anyone to do things on behalf of others, but each person must attain the awareness of the return of Christ Consciousness and our divinity and humanity.

- Christ lives in our light body.

- During the forty days after resurrection, Jesus demonstrated to His disciples (apostles) that He cannot save anyone and no one can save humanity. Each person must attain this path on his or her own, as this is the Cosmic Law.

- He demonstrated to His disciples how it is like to experience Christ consciousness.

- He expanded His light body to envelope His disciples to be elevated to the frequencies of His consciousness, enabling them to preach the gospel of truth, heal, and deliver people from cores and causes of misused energy.

- Jesus and Mary Magdalene demonstrated this truth and accomplished their missions.

- Jesus and Mary Magdalene anchored the Divine Matrix and the archetypes of the Return of Mother God. He modelled the path of Divine Love, which was His true purpose.

- After forty days of His crucifixion, He lifted his light body that has been radiated over the disciples and this left them vulnerable to fear, doubt and all the lower energies of the density of duality. During this demonstration, the disciples realised that indeed they could save themselves and not what they had been foretold.

- During the ten days after Jesus' Ascension, the disciples battled without the light of Christ that had been lifted for them to attain this path of light on their own.

- On the tenth day or the fiftieth day after crucifixion, they went to the Upper Room, which is a representation of the highest state of consciousness, being in Oneness with God.

By going into this state, the following was demonstrated and achieved:

- They consecrated their lives to the path of Oneness and Divine love.

- The baptism of sacred fire instead of water was activated.

- Their heart Chakras were opened.

- A perfect balance between the right- and left-brain hemispheres was made.

- Their Spiritual Crown Chakra was opened.

- They invoked the return of Mother God.

- They each reconnected with their I AM Presence.

- They regained their Christ Consciousness through the Sacred Fire; and

- They were each given the gifts of tongues that enabled them to travel across the face of the earth and teach the truth of Mother God; the divinity of humanity; the path of Oneness; and Divine love in the language of people they spoke to. This eliminated the language barriers and ensured the clarity of Jesus and Mary Magdalene's message.

The above is a demonstration of the success of the Divine mission of the Avatars of the Piscean Age, Jesus, and Mary Magdalene. However, all these truths were misconstrued in order to block humanity from attaining its divinity and the books that are witnesses to this truth were taken out of the Bible by the powers of Ego and patriarchy.

The notion of patriarchy and Ego has imposed itself in human relationships in order to control. It has divided humanity to the point of hatred and unforgiveness. It is the very notion that has created lack of tolerance for one another resulting in separation of minds, hearts, and Oneness of Divine love.

The walls of separateness need to be brought down through the awakening of humanity towards attaining Christ Consciousness. The path of Oneness of Divine Love is experiencing heaven on earth. It does not require people to die in their physical bodies to experience heaven, but manifests it right in this lifetime.

It is by breaking the walls of illusions of "them and us" "his fault" or "her fault". It is not one partner's responsibility to build a marriage. The manifestation of Christ Consciousness means living in your light body and radiating that light on your surroundings and all humanity.

The world depends on the demonstration of unconditional love. Love makes you rise above all dross, misconceptions, illusions, hatred, unforgiveness, anger, and many other lower energy thought forms and actions. It gives you victory over yourself.

By mastering self through Divine love, you will not react to the third dimensional world, but live in the fifth dimension–heaven on earth– while you are in this lifetime. It makes you the anchorage of peace and love in your home, your community, your city or town, your country and your continent.

By discarding the lies you have been fed lifetime after lifetime, you can start living your truth that Jesus and Mary Magdalene and many other Avatars before them successfully demonstrated, yet are suppressed by ego and patriarchy. For guidance and advice seek within your inner self/heart there you'll find truth. and advice but within your inner self.

CHAPTER SIX

THE DIVINE LOVE OF GOD

Let us look back again at God, the Creator and His consciousness. He operates within a space of peacefulness, calm, and love. He is Peace, Calm and Love, He is I AM. God does not operate in chaos, noise, anxiety, doubt, fear, judgement, unforgiveness, and all aspects of density. Your relationship with Him should be governed by unconditional love. It is the love of impersonal, constructive service to life. The God Virtue of Love, beloved Elohim Orion and His Divine Complement Angelica comes into the fore here bringing peace to the Earth through Divine love.

Without pure Divine love emanating from the heart of an individual, no lasting peace can manifest. Divine love is a positive quality, not negative sentimentality, and its radiation brings forth warmth to someone who is unhappy or imprisoned.

The Divine will of our Heavenly Father is that people learn how to love one another. Love is the cohesive power of the Universe, whether we refer to form, personal possession, or planetary peace.

Beloved Elohim Orion (God's Virtue of Love) tells us, "I come into the atmosphere of Earth on wings of Divine Love, bringing with me the concentrated flame of that Love." This Flame has been the magnetic power which drew into being the Earth upon which you stand, the very physical bodies in which you function and every other manifestation. Every form which you enjoy is part of this flame, held together by the flame of Love, for if Divine Love (which is cohesion) would cease to be, the entire universe would return to the unformed and become again part of primal life.

If you know of any life stream in this earth with whom you are not in complete accord, consciously draw the image of that person in your mind's eye now and let me give you the pressure of my feeling of unconditional loving forgiveness toward that person. If you accept this, it will set you free from the recoil of the energies of past mistakes, which made enmity in the beginning.

Love is as simple as that and yet far more complex. Every one of us yearns to feel its fullness. We need unconditional love from each other, especially spouses, family, and friends. Human beings have made love conditional and dependent on what the other person is willing to give, for example, attention or protection.

How can you truly love another person if you are always placing conditions on that "love"? As you work with these conditions, you unconsciously build obstacles to your own ability to receive and reciprocate real and unconditional love.

Why is unconditional love so elusive to many? It does not judge or distinguish between any living beings that step into its vicinity. It is love that encompasses all creation. It emanates from the heart of our Father-Mother God, from the Source of Creation, from that which created matter and placed it in the dark matter of the expanding Universe. Remember in Genesis the Bible says in the beginning the world had no form and there was only darkness and God said, "Let there be light."

Unconditional love is beyond the comprehension of the mind, which can package and divide, qualify and categorise. It surpasses any understanding; it is pure, whole, and unsullied. It is the essence of your higher self; the true essence of yourself stripped of all that is not self. (Council of Nine, Eliza Ayres https://www.thestarseedhighway.com Love flows from the heart of Creation, but you cannot feel this connection or flow with the Sources until you have connected to the Source of love within your own heart centre.

We have more than one heart. A heart that beats rhythmically, a wondrous organic pump moving oxygenated blood throughout the cardiovascular system. It feeds the cells and removes the used blood and cellular waste through the lymph system and the lungs. Human bodies are a marvellous creation made up of particles of love, blessed by the elementals and angelic beings who attend your every breath, thought, and heartbeat.

The second heart- the seat of the soul- rests within our etheric body, which is the Divine blueprint for the body that each person wears every day. The high heart is above and within the thymus gland. This heart centre is sealed in those who have not yet awakened to protect the treasure that lies within (Mathew 6 verse 19-20). It opens in response to one's efforts to open and align our energy centres.

Human bodies are a marvellous creation made up of particles of love, blessed by the elementals and angelic beings who attend your every breath, thought, and heartbeat.

The earth is a classroom and has been for a very long time. The classroom is tough because most people who are in it have not experienced love from others or themselves; however, that process is changing, the future of the planet earth is being given the opportunity to experience what actual love is. Love will be available for all who choose or are chosen to come here.

In our unique cultures, we have regarded self-love to be a selfish way of existence. We have been made to obey and look up to our family, community, and country leaders, experts in every field, religious mentors, and teachers. We have been made to look everywhere for guidance and advice.

If you are to progress in your spiritual journey, take the route less travelled. You must be willing to drop all self-criticism and face yourself. Look into your eyes and heart, and see what is at your core. If you allow yourself to look without judgement or expectation, you may surprise yourself and find that at your core, you are love and have always been.

THE DIVINE VIRTUE OF GRATITUDE

Gratitude is a virtue of God, expressed through Arch Angel Chamuel and beloved Charity and their legions of Angels of Love. It is the open door to greater benefits from God, His messengers and humanity. It opens the door for even greater blessings to occur through the experiences of the individual.

A sincere feeling of gratitude silently sent forth, or audibly expressed, is a "magic key", which can be used in developing the God-potential of every man. Let us not confuse flattery (which is insincere) with honest gratitude.

Saint Germain says: "Gratitude for the small blessings of daily life builds a momentum, which gives a person a wider perspective regarding the innumerable gifts which are constantly poured out coming in the form of challenges, for his personal benefit. Life should be a constant Prayer of Thanksgiving."

Not only on one day of the year should man give a cursory glance at the surrounding benefits, but also daily. His heart should swell with sincere gratitude just for possessing the gift of life; all of us who have arisen to the Ascended Master Octave, live in a consciousness of constant thanksgiving to God.

CHAPTER SEVEN

ACCEPTANCE OF YOUR REALITY

The damage caused by those who hate themselves, whether male or female, is deep and far-reaching. The unfortunate effect is that hatred towards self is projected to others to fill the hole within one's being. Those who loath themselves feel uncomfortably different and confused, and some are too scared to talk freely about it because they fear that they will be ridiculed. They feel as if they no longer fit into society and the life they built with pain.

Then there are those who are afraid to feel with their human hearts. They are so afraid to acknowledge that maybe in the past they were wrong; they failed or made mistakes, so instead, they resort to anger and violence. They do not understand that they need to see their past so they can heal. Only then will they be ready to embrace changes and start living better lives.

Acceptance is part of soul growth. It is an important part of your evolution. It is a growing up step. To angels it is simple; to you, it may be the biggest obstacle, as it may be difficult for you to accept your past and the misfortunes that characterise it. Consciously accepting all that has happened to you in this lifetime, good or bad, will enable you to create a better life experience. It will weaken all energy barricades that you have built to protect yourself. It will make you a better healer.

Forgiveness follows acceptance. To accept your past or current situation, you need to know what went wrong. You need not understand the person who did you wrong, or why it happened. All you need is to acknowledge that it was not right and then set your anger aside. Do not see yourself as a victim; it is as simple as it sounds. Just acknowledge and accept it. If you were the one who was wrong and feel you want to change your life, then accept and take responsibility for everything you have done. You cannot run away from it, because it will eventually catch up with you. Instead, accept what you have done and plan how you will bring light to this world to balance your karma.

Acceptance does not mean giving up. It means you have to surrender, take your power back, and leave the past in the past. It does not mean burning the bridges. It means clean them up with love and light so they may shine. When you clean up your path, you empower yourself a million times. I can hear many of you say, "But it was not fair!" Please know that you have chosen your suffering and roles in the lives you have lived, prior to each incarnation. Unfortunately, it may sound painful and unfair, but this is your script, your contract, and it will play out just as you have written it.

Many of your unpleasant experiences have led you to your awakening point so you may begin your Earth mission. It is important for you to know that you have the power to change or alter your pre-destined life by taking steps towards your natural spiritual evolution, by embracing your mission, and living your life in love and light. The future is not set in stone.

You have been reincarnated during a very exciting time of changes. Many of you dislike all the signs of awakening your consciousness and remembering who you are. We (the Angelic Realm) understand that remembering all the hurt and pain may overwhelm your nervous system and that it can temporarily hold you down, causing you depression, anxiety, panic attacks, and unhappiness. We see that you try to find answers to your problems, and therefore we are assisting you on the energy level to set your energy for global acceptance.

Global acceptance starts with each individual working with their own energy and then connecting it with other like-minded evolved individuals, thus creating soul groups. Many of you currently focus on exploring your past lives and how they have affected your current life. First, we would like you to examine your current life; ask yourself the following questions:

1. What do I need to accept?
2. What holds me down?
3. Is the energy of my unhappiness as strong as I think it is?
4. Do I want to be a victim or I want to take my energy and my power back?
5. Is it necessary to carry this emotional baggage with me all the time?

This is not the time to blame anyone about what has happened to you, but to see what is inside of you, what holds you down, and what you can release.

Do not turn your anger and fear into guilt, and vice versa. Break the pattern. All past life experiences, joyful or sad, have shaped you into the unique individual you are today.

ACCEPTING YOURSELF–EXERCISE

1. Look at yourself in the mirror; look deep into your own eyes. The eyes are the doorway to the soul.
2. See yourself for who you are, not who you were, and who you want to be. Just stop for a moment to look at yourself and acknowledge who you are. There is no right or wrong. It does not matter if you are rich or poor, healthy or sick, good or bad. Now is the moment to accept your very own self, to take stock of the journey and acknowledge the pain you have endured until now. Look at yourself and feel good about yourself. You do not need any acceptance from others. You do not need forgiveness at this moment. This moment is about you and realising how far you have come.
3. While standing in front of the mirror, looking into your soul, acknowledge that you have reached this moment, because all the circumstances of your life, good and bad, have led you to it.

4. If you are standing there, looking at yourself, hating your life and your deep wounds, then look again. Look into your eyes. You reached this point in your life, because you are ready for change; you are consciously ready. Now you can create a new reality so you can change your life pattern and create a much happier one.

5. Accept your life consciously, in your heart and mind. Some would say, "Forget everything and start all over." Instead, accept all that has happened to you and move on. Illuminate your path with love and light instead of burning it. The Lord will, hand in hand with your guides, assist you on an energy level to deal with your past and embrace your future. You have volunteered to come to Earth, and Heaven has volunteered to assist you in understanding your mission, journey, and purpose. Acceptance is just one-step. You are the creator of your happiness.

Do not turn your anger and fear into guilt, and vice versa. Break the pattern. All past life experiences, joyful or sad, have shaped you into the unique individual you are today.

CHAPTER EIGHT

THE TRUTH ABOUT CREATION

I wish to dwell more on this topic of the Oneness within all of us. As part of the company of heaven, we serve our Father Mother God. Therefore, who is this self and how does one relate to it? I want you, the reader, to expand your awareness to know more truth about Creation. None of us stands alone; we are all multi-dimensional.

People have been bantered about in reference to the need for them to awaken to the Christ Light that is within them. They must acknowledge and receive the support for continual remembrance as they expand the truth of their radiant beings as Christed Ones within the Divine Plan. We are all here to fulfil Divine contracts made before our Creator.

As I mentioned above, humanity exists in various beautiful forms. This is accepted knowledge within the higher spirals of Creation. We come in all forms, shapes, and sizes. If one chooses to incarnate within a specific star system, we refer to this as being from a specific "species". The term "species" is an expression of the beautiful myriad of humanity within and throughout Creation.

Within each species, those who incarnate within each star system are given a choice to come forth within three different Kingdoms. The two main kingdoms are Angelic and Elohim. Together, they birthed the great Cosmic Kingdom. Each kingdom has its specific qualities. Yet indeed all of the three kingdoms of the untold numbers of species are human. We are all born of the Light of Kristos, and we are in Oneness with the God Self.

As you remember the truth about our radiant being and the Oneness of all life, let us flow as one within this most delightful adventure that all shadows of illusion shall become a distant memory.

SOUL

Your soul is a part of the soul family that incarnated (at this time) on earth alongside you. Before you agreed to come to earth to assist in her evolution, you had made plans to meet and reunite with your soul family as well. The reason for incarnating you and your soul family together is to enable you to all assist one another during the time of awakening, or in times of hardship. Each one of you has a particular mission, and the ability to assist one another.

Do not allow people to take advantage of your kindness when you are assisting them. Imagine yourself as a being of light. Your intention is to send the light to your soul family so they can find you. You came here for a reason. Sometimes you may feel lost, and the challenges of life may diminish your energy. We acknowledge that life on earth is not easy; however, once you begin consciously connecting with your soul family, what you think is unbearable will become easy to bear.

Your story of suffering and healing may help someone else overcome their own suffering. Your joy and happiness may inspire others; your healing, psychic, and other abilities may help someone else understand their own. Shine your soul light to others like you so you can find one another. Be the magnet, be the lighthouse for those who are lost. If you need help or you are lost, ask that your light finds and connects you with the lighthouse.

Ask that your soul be united with other souls to show you the way and guide you during this lifetime. If you are looking for a soul mate, send your unconditional love to your soul mate so she or he may follow the illuminated energy path to find you.

Be the light that shines out and be ready for your soul family to connect with you by listening to your soul as it whispers the essence of your true self, and the slow but steady conscious transformation.

Imagine your physical body as a vehicle you use for transportation and the choices you can make. Most cars that run on gas, pollute the earth on a large scale, break easily, and corrode. Their life expectancy is short, and as they get older, they eventually have recurring problems. Now imagine a car running on solar power. It is clean, efficient, has a longer life expectancy, and in addition, it does not pollute the environment.

Your soul is the engine to your body; gas represents low vibration energy- shame, guilt, despair, grief, desire, anger, hate, and pride. Solar power symbolises higher vibration energy- trust, willingness, acceptance, forgiveness, understanding, love, joy, peace, and enlightenment- that helps your soul to heal and grow. The choice is always yours.

A connection with higher dimensions is always available when you take care of your body and soul. When your soul discovers that dimensions can operate on solar power, you are healing your soul. Communication with beings of light and telepathy will become natural and you will rediscover many natural and wonderful gifts you have been blessed with.

Healing yourself opens the door to transformation. Cosmic and spiritual energy are constantly available to all of us. When you reach its frequency, you consciously connect to higher dimensions while you are still in the physical body. This is a very slow process. Your guides may communicate with you, or you may find a true teacher on earth; true teachers are rare to find, but they exist. Self spiritual work, discipline and love will all be your companions on this journey.

While you are going through soul healing and transformation, you will re-open a part of yourself that you have consciously forgotten. You may encounter many fears along the way. When this happens, put your hands on your stomach (your third chakra) and feel those fears. You can never outrun them, but they will not harm you as long as you are aware that they are there and see them for what they are. Address them peacefully, right within your third chakra and your emotional body.

While I am exploring this topic of self-healing, let me borrow from one exceptional book I stumbled upon while the Lord was busy with my healing. I will refer to a portion that explains our origin and purpose and how we were created. The book was written by Werner Schroeder compiled from The Teachings of the Bridge to Freedom:

THE SEVEN BODIES

1. I AM PRESENCE AND THE THREEFOLD FLAME

The I AM Presence is the individualised focus of God, connected to the heart of the physical body through the silver cord. It is the real you, the being through which you will function after you have achieved your self-mastery. It is the God within you that knows only perfection and is ever pouring forth; it is expanding. It is your permanent self that never dies.

The individualised focus has the potential power of Godparents.

The I AM Presence can think and create from primal life what it desires using free will.

When you first came to the planet, Earth the glorious presence filled the entire form, which you then wore. That God Presence enfolded in the Threefold Flame; it was visible to all men. Through the rhythm of that flame, you were able to draw from universal light substance any form you desired. In addition, by the magnetic power of the coalescing action of the flame you could design and precipitate food, clothing, shelter, temples, and anything you desired or needed. Through the power of your feelings, which energised these thought forms, these manifestations took place instantly.

What happened to that Magnificent Presence when attention no longer rested on God's Presence but focused on human creation? The flame within the heart decreased in size and influence. In the average spiritually awakened individual, this flame is now less than one-sixteenth of a centimetre in height.

As that flame in the heart is now fed by your attention and love which is your life, it will increase in size. This focus of God perfection is anchored within the physical heart of every individual. It functions in the physical body and is composed of three beautiful plumes of brilliant flame- blue on the left (representing energy, which becomes power through use), gold- the centre plume (representing wisdom and illumination) and the pink plume representing Divine love on the right.

When a person acknowledges and invokes the presence of God, it always fills the individual with light.

I live, move and have my being in the very presence of God. I cannot lift a finger except by using the life of that presence. I cannot speak a word, but for that presence.

If you consecrate your mind and feelings to remember the actual presence of God, then you shall be a light bearer to the world.

2. THE CAUSAL BODY

All the constructively qualified energy gathered during all your embodiments is contained in the great reservoir of good and perfection shown as seven concentric circles of colour around the I AM presence. This is known as the "causal body" and within this body The Treasures in Heaven, which cannot be stolen or decay, are stored. This is mentioned in Matthew 6 v 20-21: "But lay up for yourselves treasures in heaven where neither moth nor rust consumes, and where thieves don't break through and steal; for where your treasure is, there your heart will be also."

The causal body contains the "accumulated good"; the opposite of Karma which is the energy qualified in a harmonious manner. The causal body of each individual is built through eons of time, starting with the time we passed through the Seven Spheres.

Even when out of embodiment, dwelling in inner spheres, we are adding to the good of this causal body. Thus, you can see not all causal bodies are alike. The band of the colour of the sphere in which we spent the largest amount of time will be the largest around the causal body.

It determines the ray to which you as an individual belong. We can often discover the ray to which we belong by asking ourselves what our favourite colour is. The individual may be on two rays, one of them being dominant. Advanced students may be on several rays.

There is an additional service the causal body performs when only 51% of the energy of the individual is qualified with perfection. That energy anchored within the causal body acts as a magnet assisting the life stream to ascend. Thus, the causal body becomes the cause of the self-mastery from whence comes the name.

3. THE CHRIST SELF

When the individual applied for embodiment, the Christ Self came into being. This Christ Self is the provision that the I AM Presence has made to assist us in the human world. It is a replica (in a form) of the I AM Presence but vibrates at a lower rate. The Christ Self abides in a position between I AM Presence and the physical body. It regulates the amount of energy flowing through the silver cord. Because it operates at a lower vibration, it is aware of imperfections such as disease but does not take it on and accept it.

The Christ Self is aware of what we are doing and whatever our needs are and it takes those needs to I AM Presence. Therefore, the Christ Self functions as a step-down transformer.

The Christ Self is the directing intelligence through which the presence works. It guides the individual in a particular embodiment. It is the still small voice within which we also call "the guardian angel"; it sometimes gives promptings to do certain things. The number of promptings is usually three, and if we do not follow these promptings, they are discontinued after the third time.

4. THE MENTAL BODY

The Mental Body was formed out of the substance of the air. It was designed to be the chalice for the receptivity of Divine ideas. It has the power to mould these ideas into a workable form. The mind, also called consciousness, is contained in the mental body. The mental body was created to be the instrument to hold a pattern, or vision of perfection; to build the form of what you desire to manifest, holding it until the feelings energise it for physical manifestation.

Humanity has used this process in reverse by holding in the mind pictures of imperfections like fear, failure, and judgement they end up manifesting.

Your mental body receives through your attention all activities of the senses and everything that your attention connects with (good or evil). It draws back the picture and forms into your mind. The mental bodies of mankind are like an old warehouse where old furniture has been stored for ages.

They are full of cobwebs and discordant human concepts, some of which are in the process of disintegration.

When you first received these mental bodies from the heart of Creation, they were like crystal balls of light into which clear conscience and beautiful ideas and patterns from your own Holy Christ Self were given.

If the mental body is not purified, it cannot receive the perfect design from the Godhead or other holy benevolent beings. It cannot manifest the strength to hold that design against the disintegrating forces of doubt, fear, ridicule, and many other negative qualities in the atmosphere of Earth. These qualities always endeavour to destroy a constructive pattern.

Be careful of what you invite to be the guests of your mental body for the next twenty-four hours. Change your habits, thoughts, feelings, and what you speak.

5. THE EMOTIONAL BODY

The emotional body is the largest of the four lower bodies (consisting of the emotional, mental, etheric, and physical bodies). It contains the world of our feelings.

Its function is to nourish Divine ideas with positive feelings of accomplishment and every virtue of happiness, purity, mercy, forgiveness, and peace.

When the emotional body was created, it comprised electrons drawn from the emotional realm, the realm of feelings, the realm of angels, and the archangels.

Your emotional body comprises millions of tiny electrons in constant movement. These form atoms. If the motion of electrons is in accord with the rhythm of your God flame and the constructive radiation of some master, that is fine.

The emotional body will deflect all destructive feelings, and discordant energy projected at you. You are then the master of all energy wherever you are.

6. THE ETHERIC BODY AND THE SOUL

The etheric body contains the memories of all past deeds, thoughts, and feelings during former embodiments–both good and evil. The accumulation of these records is called "the soul".

The etheric body, therefore, is the envelope of the soul. When an individual is not in the embodiment, he lives in his etheric body and has the consciousness of the soul.

If discordant energies have caused wounds or tears in the etheric body, these wounds are healed and patched over by nature, but the scars remain. In uncertain circumstances or during similar experiences, when undue pressure is exerted on that scar by similar experiences, it acts like an incision. It gives way, bursts open, and manifests as disease, distress, or disharmony.

Deep feelings definitely make a record on the etheric body.

The etheric body is one most closely connected to the physical, and it is the one in which you travel at night when you sleep. So the more purified and sensitive to divinity that etheric body is, the easier it is (when that etheric body slips up back into and around the physical body) to remember the Divine truths and joyful experiences that take place at the inner levels. It also becomes easy to know the joy of being in the presence of the Divine beings and bringing that association back into the world of form.

When you relive repeatedly the distressing events of the past, you energise them again to act in your present world. This is why in recounting the history of humankind, the masters never told of the destructive records of wars and injuries to physical bodies.

If the etheric body, which contains the etheric consciousness, is not purified, failures of the past that are recorded there will often neutralise or destroy the desired form before it can be externalised for the blessings of life.

Call upon the Law of Forgiveness for your misuse of life throughout the ages, and accept the gift of purity from the Elohim Claire (God's aspect of purity) so you may see, know, and become a perfect expression of your own individualised I AM Presence- a holy grail. You will receive into your outer mind the Divine ideas from that presence, which through your purified centres of thought, feelings and spoken word, you can externalise for your own blessing and for the benefit of your fellowman.

Within every electron released from the heart of God, is the power to create and sustain the kingdom of heaven for yourself, your family, your world and the students entrusted to your loving care, right here on earth. Within the brazier of your heart, you carry the most powerful concentrate of the "atomic accelerator"; you have full and free access to all that we are and all that we have.

7. THE PHYSICAL BODY

The physical body provides the anchorage to the earth. It is the vehicle through which man functions and expands the borders of God's Kingdom into a lower vibratory plane.

The physical body, therefore, is the temple of the living God. "Do you not know that our bodies are a temple of the Holy Spirit, who is in you, whom you have received from God?" (1 (Corinthians 6v19). Originally, this body was not as dense as it is now. It vibrated at a much higher level and it comprised what we would today call "etheric substance".

Humanity, as it existed during the first Golden Age, would appear as etheric, misty shadowy beings but of identical form as humankind today.

The silver cord enters the physical body at the top of the head (the soft spot of a newborn baby) and provides the connection to the Christ Self and I AM Presence.

It is the life-giving, life-maintaining fountain of energy. If left without this fountain of life force, the physical body cannot operate and death would ensue.

The brain is the physical organ through which the mind functions. It generates impressions from the outer world and is the vehicle of the mind.

By the correct use of the name of God, and cleansing his four lower bodies through the use of the Violet Flame, man may build his new world, and attain eternal mastery in the victory of his self-mastery into Light. This is the immortal goal of every life stream of this planet or any other–the self-mastery into the Light.

The Ascended Master, Jesus Christ, accomplished this victory and attained His own self-mastery by faithfully using the same laws that He and the other Great Ones are teaching us today. Did He not say: "The things I have done shall ye do also?"

The inner vehicles (physical body) of the individual house, the causes and cores of imperfection. The physical body will express perfection when such perfection is expressed in all lower bodies (emotional, mental, etheric, and physical).

Elohim Claire's Divine compliment, Lady Astrea's services comprise the purification of the astral realm-which extends to about 3.048km above earth, where cores of impurity and evil exist. She has helped to remove the psychic substance contained within the atmosphere of the earth. She has also removed and destroyed destructive forces and vortices. She accomplishes this by encircling humanity's created discord (psychic substance) around persons, places, conditions, and things with a sword of blue flame, holding the impurity leashed until it can be dissolved and transmuted into perfection.

On this subject, beloved Astrea addresses students as follows:

"I have offered to remove the causes and cores of all known and unknown impurities in the life stream belonging to this earth and all individuals may demand the fulfilment of that from me now."

"I stand ready to always use the circle and sword of the blue flame to cut away the imperfections upon this planet, and the legions of purity on the fourth ray are waiting for the commands of human beings and can go into action in an instant; they have no limit. But the demand for this service must be made from unascended mankind."

"I have offered to remove the causes and cores of all known and unknown impurities in the life stream belonging to this earth and all individuals may demand the fulfilment of that from me now."

"Beloved, you are responsible to the Cosmic Law for the use of your God-given energy. When we present an existing condition to you which must be remedied through the use of the Sacred Fire, in the name of all that is God and Holy Spirit, go into action and make your demand upon for the release of the purifying fires which remove the causes and cores of imperfection."

The above illustration gives us a bit of understanding of who we really are and how to deal with thoughts, feelings, and circumstances we face in our daily lives. More knowledge and understanding lessen the anger, hatred, and unforgiveness that humanity carries unnecessarily, thus delaying the process of self-mastery to the light of God.

CHAPTER NINE

UNDERSTANDING HUMANITY AND WHAT WE ARE MADE UP OF

Identifying our misconceptions can be challenging. We do not always perceive things as they really are, because what we take in goes through a filter of our emotional and mental matrix.

Rumi says, "'Lo I AM with you always means when you look for God, God is in the look of your eyes, nearer to you than yourself."

And Aungsan Suu Kyi asserts: "If we can learn or as we learn to distance ourselves from our prejudices when assessing a situation, the search for truth has to be accompanied by awareness."

If you are aware of what you are doing, you have an objective view of yourself. And if you are aware of what other people are doing, you become more objective about them. For example, awareness means that when you are aware of the fact that somebody is shouting at you, do not think to yourself "what a horrible person"; that is purely subjective. However, if you are aware, you know that the person is shouting, because he or she is angry or frightened; that is objectivity. Without awareness, all kinds of prejudices multiply. Humour can help us to develop objectivity, but a sense of humour requires a certain amount of objectivity in a situation. This is why it is healthy.

In addition to the above statement, we are demanded to let go of our pride, our Ego, and aloofness and find a way to make our spirituality practical and all-embracing. The negative vibrational quality of pride can create a dark and gloomy corona around the head of an individual rather than a brilliant yellow corona of the illumined ones. This dark energy can obliterate our contact with the higher mind, making it even harder to receive the impulses of the Divine through the crown chakra. The rite of passage that we face at the level of our crown chakra also demands that we appreciate others and learn from everyone. One of the signs of the emerging spirituality of our era is an appreciation of diversity.

As we move into the future, we can learn so much from one great emperor – Akba the Great, a sixteenth-century mogul emperor, a great military genius and a wise ruler. His main desire was to reconcile the diversity of the religious creed that he saw before him- Christianity, Muslim, Hinduism, Zoroastrian, and Judaism.

He was the first monarch in his medieval age to recognise that there was truth in all religions, which we cannot do today. This encouraged him to create his own monotheistic universal religion called The Divine Faith. His goal was to bring about unity amid diversity. Beloved, these paths are more alike than they are different and this is the reality with so many things in life. We can enjoy diversity and even benefit from it while seeking the underlying unity.

While expounding on adversity the following are diverse spiritual qualities of each individual embodied on Mother Earth. The ray represents the colour and virtue of God Head. As a being is prepared for earth to live in human form, he or she passes several rays for initiation and preparation, and the ray they find to be much more connected with or saturated in becomes their area of speciality and choice. The representatives are the higher beings operating from the other two kingdoms of the God Head-the Angelic Kingdom and the Elohim Kingdom. The Masters are those beings who once incarnated on earth in the human form and passed all their initiations by mastering Self in obedience to the wisdom of God Head and are now called "The Ascended Masters". We who are on earth awakening to Self and Christ Consciousness are called "Intergrated Ascended Masters".

RAY 1:

Colour blue.

REPRESENTATIVE MASTER /ELOHIM/ARCHANGEL:

Beloved El Morya, Elohim Hercules, and Archangel Michael.

Doing the will of God, illumined faith, and capacity to lead people and manifest large amounts of energy, and initiative. All of God's ideas are born here.

Distinctive attribute of the undeveloped individual: Aggressive human will and domination.

RAY 2:

Colour Sunshine yellow

REPRESENATIVE MASTER/ ELOHIM/ ARCHANGEL/

BELOVED LORD: Lanto, Elohim Cassiopea, and Archangel Jophiel. Perception, illumination, and inspiration. Ideas are perceived and moulded into thought patterns and workable form. Wisdom and discrimination.

Distinctive attribute of undeveloped individual: Intellectual arrogance, accretion of worldly knowledge.

RAY 3:

Colour pink

REPRESENTATIVE MASTER /ELOHIM/ARCHANGEL:

Beloved Paul the Venetian, Elohim Orion, and Archangel Chamuel. Divine love, compassion, tolerance, and gratitude. Ideas are clothed with life essence through the feeling nature enabling future externalisation in the world of form. Love is shown as a cohesive force, holding together a manifested form.

Distinctive attribute of the undeveloped individual: Lack of love for human beings, elementals and animals.

RAY 4:

Colour White

REPRESENTATIVE MASTER /ELOHIM/ARCHANGEL:

Beloved Serapis Bey, Elohim of Purity, and Archangel Gabriel. Artistic development, humility, holding to Immaculate Concept.

Distinctive attribute of undeveloped individual: Lust, passion, arrogance, negative criticism and gossip.

RAY 5:

Colour Emerald green

REPRESENTATIVE MASTER/ELOHIM/ARCHANGEL: Beloved

Hilarion, Elohim Vista and Archangel Raphael.

Scientific development, healing, concentration and consecration, and searching for the highest truth.

Distinctive attribute of undeveloped individual: Doubt, discouragement, lack of discipline and atheistic tendencies.

RAY 6:

Colour: Ruby with golden radiance

REPRESENTATIVE MASTER /ELOHIM/ARCHANGEL:

Beloved Lady Nada, Elohim of Peace and Archangel Uriel. Unselfish service away from home.

Distinctive attribute of undeveloped individual: Religious fanaticism and zealous tendencies.

RAY 7

Colour Violet

REPRESENTATIVE MASTER /ELOHIM/ARCHANGEL:

Beloved Saint Germaine, Elohim Arcturus, and Archangel Zadkiel. Ceremonial service, culture, refinements, master of circumstances and diplomacy.

Distinctive attribute of undeveloped individual: Lack of refinement and snobbery.

Each individual embodied is either is in one of these rays currently or has been before in the past or future embodiments depending on his or her choice.

Many people are not living according to their true purpose, which has been demonstrated to them.

However, the purpose of the above illustration is to give the reader an idea of how to be objective while reacting to the behaviour of an undeveloped individual. These characteristics play out in any kind of relationship. The illustration may assist in changing the perspective of the reader.

Appreciating and accepting the diversity of others can assist individuals to deal with circumstances around them and avoid a separation from the Oneness that many have fallen into.

To become such a master presence, the threefold nature of man must be nurtured and developed. The cosmic cycle was instituted and sustained to the present day.

I am not saying it is going to be easy, but exercising caution and discernment will help to lighten the load. It is more about learning to master ourselves first before we master others and trying to change them which may result in discord and division.

Our planet was created to give each individual evolving upon it an opportunity to realise their spiritual nature and become master of energy and vibration through the conscious control and use of their creative faculties. To become such a master presence, the threefold nature of man must be nurtured and developed. The cosmic cycle was instituted and sustained to the present day.

As each new minor cycle opens, a new method of incorporating the energies of people is presented to embodied individuals. This is done through the kind assistance of a representative of the Chohan Avatar who is head of the active Ray (Like Jesus who is the head of the sixth ray, the Age of Pisces). This representative is always an unascended being who has been closely associated with the Chohan during past incarnations and also between embodiments. In his inner bodies he is well-acquainted with the Chohan's ray and service.

Avatar is a being who like Jesus has worked his karma prior to his incarnation and is, therefore, a pure channel through which the finest essence of the ray is incorporated into the activities of the new religion.

Before and after his coming, the work is left in the hands of the dedicated individuals who explain the law as their consciousness sees it.

We are in this before stage, and the forerunners of Seventh Ray (Age of Acquarius, the current age) activity have done well. Unfortunately, they have not touched even the periphery of the truth concerning the power of invoking, wielding, and dispensing the spiritual currents that are the Seventh Ray's gifts for the upliftment of the race.

CHAPTER TEN

UNDERSTANDING FREEDOM: GODS PERSPECTIVE

Beloved Saint Germaine

Does your inner self cry out for some sort of freedom that seems to be more than decades away from you? Let's first understand what this freedom is.

Who are our authentic self and the power of one? Let's discover our full and original purpose. Let's understand what our Divine plan is. What is God's original purpose of marriage?

From the cradle to grave, as a human being you are bombarded with energies and ideas that are designed to prevent you from exercising your co-creative powers in making this planet a godlier place. You are being programmed to be passive, to live like all other people, to think that you cannot make a difference, that you do not have the power to change your society. However, everything on this planet is determined by the free will of human beings in embodiment.

Thus, one person can make a difference by making up his or her own mind with unwavering determination, which is something that is not actually an act of will. It is an act of being, an act of being who you are, being in contact with a higher part of your being so that the light from your higher being shines through the lower mind. By doing this, you can come to a determination that is not the outer will – that can easily be shifted by the outward impulse – but it is actually an inner determination. It is the knowledge that this is the new reality on your planet because you are that change and you are willing to be the change in the world. This can be done by holding a spiritual balance for that change, so that you hold an unwavering vision for that manifestation to come.

Why is freedom so important? How does it relate to overcoming the poverty of consciousness? Well, what is the essence of poverty? Its essence is the separation from God's abundance. Well, what is the essence of anti-freedom? It is that you are separated from God; you are separated from Oneness with God.

Out of that illusion of separation countless illusions that keep you trapped in a mental box emerge, where you define borders around yourselves and say, "I am inside this mental box. All other people are outside that mental box and God is somewhere way beyond that mental box." This beloved is anti-freedom.

The separate mind, the Ego, defines freedom as the ability to do and have whatever it wants; to have all of its needs fulfilled. Indeed, in our society, even in spiritual and religious movements, the prevailing attitude is: if we can do whatever we want, then we are free. This means if we can escape the consequences of our actions, then we are free.

Many spiritual people have tried to walk the spiritual path to learn some magical formula that will allow them to do whatever they want and escape the consequences of their actions. They believe that this is freedom, but this is a completely perverted concept of freedom. It springs from the consciousness of those who have fallen into duality and thus have lost Oneness with God. It is freedom only for the separate self, but that is not true freedom. The separate self has no reality, no existence in God–and thus, how can it ever be freedom?

One needs to realise that true freedom does not mean an escape from the consequences of one's actions. It means acknowledging the reality that the physical universe is the cosmic mirror that returns to you what you send out.

If you free your mind from those illusions that spring from the consciousness of separation and lack, then you will begin to project into the cosmic mirror images and ideas that do not seek to raise the separate self but raise other people to do something for humankind. You develop a global awareness where you seek to raise all rather than the separate self. When you do this, the cosmic mirror will gladly and lovingly, as cycles go through the four levels of the material universe, reflect to you exactly what you are sending out.

Thus, you will escape the limitations that are created by the separate self and its belief that to gain, it must take from others. There is enough wealth and abundance in the material world to provide for everyone. If you shift your thinking and look at this, even with the outer logical mind, you will see that what takes away your freedom is the illusion that it is possible to gain something by taking through force instead of doing what Jesus instructed. He said, "Seek ye first the Kingdom of God and His righteousness and all these things will be added unto you."

The Kingdom of God is within you, so you seek first that inner Oneness with the higher being. When you attain it, you see that you are connected to God just as all other beings are connected to Him through their higher selves. You will realise that if you work to set other people free, God will multiply your efforts beyond anything you could attain by taking it through force in the material realm.

Literally beloved, the message Jesus brought concerned God's desire to give you infinite abundance. The condition for that provision is your willingness to share the abundance with everyone else, instead of trying to hoard it for pleasure, or for a sense of security or power or the Ego (the separate self).

When you begin to contemplate these concepts, there can be no true freedom in separation. Why is this so? Freedom can only be found in one place and that is in Oneness with your higher being; Oneness with your fellow beings; Oneness with your source; and Oneness with the infinite. You can have infinite freedom when you are one with the infinite. Freedom is truly free when it is infinite. The concept of freedom that most people have on earth is dualistic; it is always seen as the opposite of anti-freedom. In addition, many people on earth are not able to grasp the concept of infinite, non-dualistic freedom; a freedom that has no opposite, for it needs no opposite.

UNDERSTANDING FREEDOM

Many spiritual people around the world have had few experiences of true non-dualistic freedom. They have not been able to understand it, because their minds are still focused on the dualistic polarity, where you think that to be happy you have to know what it means to be unhappy, therefore, you can experience freedom only when you have experienced bondage. Such people need the contrast to know what it really means to be free or happy.

Beyond this dualistic interplay of light and darkness, there is the reality of God, which we have often called "bliss". Because people immediately start projecting their dualistic concepts and images on it, they limit it. Yet true freedom is bliss that has no opposite.

If you experience it for the first time, you may not know what to do with it. It literally takes some adjustment of overcoming the linear thinking of the outer mind before you realise that this is a state of freedom, because it can never have an opposite. Therefore, you can never be anti-free when you are in that state of being.

The state of flowing with the River of Life is called the "flow of IS". So is it God's desire to have that awareness, that experience of the reality of God that is beyond the dualistic extremes so you no longer look at the world through the filter of duality. It is however unavoidable at the present level of consciousness that when people awaken to the spiritual side of life, they are awakened to a greater awareness of both light and darkness. It is almost unavoidable that many people go through a period where they focus not only on their problems but also on those in the world.

Because of this misconception of freedom, many relationships are strained; they function on the foundation of separateness and not Oneness with God, which is true freedom.

The Lord is not pleased to see many living for 20, 30, 40 years or more being focused on the duality between light and darkness. These people never feel at peace; there is always more work to be done, more prayers to be made, more decrees or rosaries to be given. They feel like they are always behind; they are always running after the carrot that is dangling in front of their noses, but it keeps eluding them. The harder they strive to get the carrot, the faster it moves from their grasp. Because of this misconception of freedom, many relationships are strained; they function on the foundation of separateness and not Oneness with God, which is true freedom.

CHAPTER ELEVEN

DISCOVERING THE AUTHENTIC SELF AND UNDERSTANDING THE POWER OF ONE

Beloved Saint Germaine

There is a story about a messenger who was very concerned about a nuclear war. His worry had started when he was young. He went deep into meditation one night and cried out to God as he felt a great degree of Oneness with Him on the issue of nuclear war; he cried out to stop it. He felt a return current, a reassurance that there would not be a nuclear war, at least a large-scale nuclear war on this planet. Unbeknown to his outer mind was that he had vowed to contribute in holding the balance to prevent such a war.

Yet one person cannot hold the balance if millions of people pull to the opposite direction, because the law of free will must outplay itself in giving people the lessons they need to change their consciousness. While there is value in one person shifting his or her consciousness, in most issues a certain critical mass must be reached so that there is a counter balance between those who are willing to be indifferent without knowing better.

People's assertion that it only takes one student or person to change a planet is true in the sense that one person's shift in the mindset can lead to a collective consciousness in the long-term. However, it takes a certain critical mass of individuals to prevent certain outer manifestations. If one person, or just a few people, can remove an ungodly condition from this planet, how will the majority learn and come to the point where they decide that they too have had enough of that manifestation?

The power of one must be understood at different levels of consciousness. There is value in you making up your mind, but it is also necessary that you realise that you are not a separate being. You live in a world with approximately seven billion other individuals, which gives you the sense of Oneness with your own I AM Presence, but also takes you to the next step of realising your Oneness with all other people.

Thus, you realise my beloved that it is not always enough for you to come to an inner determination based on Oneness with your own higher being. It is also necessary to fulfil the Omega requirement, and go out and seek to awaken others so that they can come into Oneness with their own higher beings. The result of this is that a critical mass of people can become one on a particular issue, and therefore shift the collective consciousness.

What is true compassion? In order to answer that question, we have to make a distinction between compassion and sympathy. We tend to use those words interchangeably, but in order to understand the subtleties involved in developing the heart chakra, it helps to make this distinction: On one hand, compassion comes from our higher self and gives to another what he or she really needs at that moment. Sympathy comes from the level of the lower self and stands in the space of what the souls really need.

Sympathy allows us to feel sorry for ourselves, to indulge our weaknesses, to slide into a "woe is me" slump. Sympathy validates that sense that we have been victimised rather than helping us to see our challenges as opportunities.

In the aura, sympathy shows up as a syrup dripping of energy from the heart and as spirals of energy moving downward, which eventually drag down the emotions and soul awareness. Compassion dips into the pure fires of the heart to uplift others so they can realise their full potential. It supports the process of soul refinement. Sympathy can be overbearing or smothering rather than supportive.

Compassion does not leave someone who is hurting where it found him. It's ok to support a child, a friend or a loved one, but when our caring cushions them from learning their lessons and growing from them, we are not doing them any favour. Sometimes those we love the most need a dose of reality, a wake–up call.

Sympathy validates that sense that we have been victimised rather than helping us to see our challenges as opportunities.

We cannot force a flower to blossom by pulling apart its leaves or by overwatering it, but we can make sure it has enough air, water, sunlight, and food.

Having done that, we can only let go and allow the flower to flourish according to its timetable and strength. The same thing applies to the souls in our care.

Sometimes it is so hard to let go. When our children start walking, we want to guard them against getting hurt and give them the support they need. Yet it is important to let them try until they make that first step on their own. The same is true for all the steps we take in life; no one can do it for us, and we cannot do it for anyone else.

CHAPTER TWELVE

ADVANCED HEALING MECHANISM

Untamed Ego affected many people in our society. It sabotages their spiritual growth, relationships, especially marriages. It is important to note that the real you is the observer Self, who is the controller and director, the chooser and cause. The key to be the director is understanding the need to be misidentified from the content of consciousness.

You are not your thoughts, emotions, body, behaviour, actions, personality, mistakes, successes, abilities, past, future or beliefs. You are the Consciousness, not the Creation. You can direct and control only that from which you are disidentified. That which you as the consciousness or "I" are identified will be your master. Living in this world you must deal with form. Practise identifying and "disidentifying". Practise being the controller, the cause and creator of your life as you would in your role in a play.

Always remember what your real Self is, who and what you really are, not Negative Ego. Negative Ego is the result of psychological imbalances and being completely cut off from the spiritual body and possibly even from the intellectual pursuits or thoughts.

The following illustration taken from the Ascension Glossary by Lisa Rene (https://www.ascensionglossary.com) will help us to introspect in order to root out and block the Mind Control forces from stealing the joy and happiness in our relationships.

For those who feel or realise that the damage has already been done, it is never too late to heal yourself so that you can help others until the whole family is healed. The healing will go down to the community and who knows, eventually the nation and globally.

EGOTISM – THE FIRST STAGES

Egotism is the drive to maintain and enhance favourable views about oneself and features an inflated opinion of one's personal features and importance–intellectual, physical, social, and others. Egotism describes a person who acts to gain more than what he or she gives to others. It means placing oneself at the core of the one's world with no concern for others, including those one loves or considers as "close".

NARCISSISM–THE SECONDARY STAGES

Narcissism is a disorder in which a person has an inflated sense of self-importance. It is caused by a combination of genetic and environmental factors.

PSYCHOPATHY—THE THIRD AND FINAL STATES OF INSANITY

Psychopathy as a personality disorder is characterised by enduring anti-social behaviour, diminished empathy and remorse, and a disinhibited or bold behaviour. Behaviourists suggest that different conceptions of psychopathic behaviour emphasise three main characteristics to varying degrees: Low fear of consequences, poor impulse control, and lack of empathy and attachment to others. All these result in cruelty and meanness.

EMOTIONAL MANIPULATION

As the chaos generated from the planetary ascension accelerates, many people are being influenced by negative forces that they do not understand and use more emotional manipulation to cope with their dismantling reality.

Some of these negative forces emanate from people's unconscious minds and negative Egos that have reinforced a lifetime of negative habits and behaviours. When people feel insecure, they will easily resort to controlling and manipulative behaviour. It is helpful to educate oneself about this behaviour for self-protection and creation of necessary healthy boundaries.

The concept of Egotism describes a person who acts to gain value for self-serving motivation and instinctual desires while taking excessive resources than what he or she gives back to others. This may also be referred to as "service to self".

Usually, these actions of taking in others' energy, time, and resources are combined with very low ethical standards and a display of low moral character traits. This is called Consumptive Modelling or Energetic Vampirism. Egotism may be fulfilled by exploiting the sympathy, trauma, emotions, or ignorance of others. It is also satisfied by using coercion, deception, manipulation, mind control, and fraud.

The Egotist has an overwhelming sense of the centrality of the "me" operating in their personal qualities and personal identity. This is a person who cannot be trusted as they will always manipulate the circumstances to serve themselves.

Without developing self-awareness and Ego discipline, the untamed negative Ego is exploited by mind control and further develops into serious spiritual pathologies that lead to narcissism and psychopathy. Psychotropic mind control harnesses the lower vibratory frequencies that comprise the lower three layers of Ego for targeting negative Ego and AD behaviours in the population.

SELF-JUSTIFICATION

Unfortunately, we are often confused by what we perceive incorrectly through our own need to be okay through self-justification. We formulate these distortions as Ego Defence Mechanism, because we have not learned how to free the mind by using negative Ego tools for self-exploration and deeper self-enquiry. As we learn to free our minds and love ourselves unconditionally, we know that we are okay without having to self–justify.

When we are freed from our own need for self-justification, by increasing our inner self-approval and self-love, no matter where we find ourselves, we are not compelled to justify others or ourselves. We are freed to be capable of loving others, no matter what they may choose to do. We have no control over what others think about us.

EGO IGNORANCE

Ignorance is defined as that which is only identified with the material world and the use of external organs of perception. To remain ignorant is a choice that many people make both consciously and unconsciously, because they are afraid. Satanic forces and the NAA understand this trauma behaviour in humanity and exploit this weakness of Ego fear aggressively.

If the masses remain in negative Ego fears, they will remain ignorant, and vulnerable to manipulation and mind control through chaos, fears, confusion, and power conflicts.

This is the time to leave fear and ignorance of Negative Ego thought patterns. You need to prevent fear from controlling you. Search for spiritual knowledge that your inner soul and heart will resonate with and lead you from darkness, ignorance, and suffering.

The biggest impediment to all humans in their quest for spiritual truth and knowledge is unresolved Ego fear, religious mind control, and emotional immaturity based on unhealed trauma.

If we have fear and believe we are not worthy enough, we stunt our development thereby refusing access to deep self-knowledge. If we refuse to get out of the superficial levels of life interaction (kiddie pool), mentally or emotionally, we remain immature to grasp higher spiritual knowledge.

This ignorance leaves most human beings dog-paddling in circles through life, completely unable to make informed decisions about the direction they should take in the future, because the controllers treat them like farm animals. Self-awareness and spiritual knowledge ultimately reach the nexus point in one's spiritual journey where the catalytic breakthrough beyond ignorance, and negative Ego is required to progress, evolve and be free.

PREDATOR MIND

The Imposter Spirit is the Satanic Spirit which promotes false light authority and anti-life architecture through deception, lies of omission, and manipulation. It uses malice to promote harm and death. These anti-life belief systems are the basis that form the negative Ego and were manifested out of the predator mind of the Orion Group.

The predator mind stays in its superiority complex of polarity while it projects inferiority on the targets of its submission and enslavement.

This is the predictability of the Orion Group and its repeated use of the controller archetype. To master the Negative Ego one needs to identify these inferior or superior thought forms and their archetypes and belief systems as they are acted upon. This helps to shift and refocus negative thoughts back into neutral.

HOW TO GUARD AGAINST OR FREE YOURSELF

- This is the act of freeing your mind from being under Mind Control. Do an inventory of personal thoughts and identify them as inferior or superior, or as love or fear thoughts. Choose thoughts you want to own and those you want to discard.

- As a goal, use the above spiritual centering model to keep your mind balanced and remain centred in loving and neutral thoughts.

- How long can you remain in the centre? Make it a goal to improve your ability to stay within the essence and energy of the keywords that maintain your spiritual centre.

- Bring yourself back to the centre with the breath, and applying neutral association to circumstances when you fall out of inner balance.

Superior Thinking attributes are:

Intolerance, impatience, arrogance, manipulation, attack, anger, and, judgemental thinking.

Inferior Thinking attributes are:

Worry, low self-love, low self-esteem, jealousy, guilt, hurt, fear, attachment, and martyrdom.

When you drop into inferior or superior thought-forms, immediately label it as Negative Ego, and do not identify with the thought as defining your value or true Christ nature. Do not let negative thoughts control you. Refocus and affirm the correct thought pattern.

STOP EGO AND SATANIC FORCES

We must be able to identify destructive patterns (Ego and fear) from healthy patterns (spiritual love) in order to make informed choices and have personal discernment. If we do not do this, we are not discerning in the quality or level of information we are being exposed to and we allow ourselves to be externally influenced by charismatic abusers, predators, manipulators, and liars.

It is important to identify abusers, liars, predators, and sociopaths as people traumatised by pain, soul fragmentation, and spiritual disconnection. Why would we give value to the words spoken in the skewed theories of a person or group member who is a serial abuser, liar, or predator? This is akin to returning to the same church to listen to sermons where the priest molests altar boys. We have to understand that such a person is very sick, in pain and disturbed.

NEGATIVE EGO IS UNTRUSTWORTHY

One can never trust a person who has a fractured Ego, a fragmented soul, and emotionally infantile no matter how charismatic they are. A person in this condition needs love, compassion, and spiritual help. This is the general profile of a wounded Ego, and definition of a being possessed by Satan. Similarly, a loving mother would never put her child in the care of a known sexual predator.

Unfortunately, there are many charismatic liars promoting themselves in positions of authority and in the spiritual consciousness realm through predator-seducer Egos and direct satanic manipulation. These people are charming. To see satanic manipulation, you have to understand its Ego motivation, strategies, and ideological reasons for exploiting human beings. It uses NAA methods like Archontic Deceptor Behaviour (a spiritually abusive behaviour that disconnects you from God and Christ).

To stop the darkness from manipulating your energy and influencing your body, you have to halt it in its tracks and always refuse its authority or control over your being in every way.

RESPONSIBILITY OF CONSENT

To stop Negative Ego, you must identify it and terminate it before it accesses your mind, emotions, body, and spirit. It takes conviction and strength to reclaim your spiritual power and body. God's authority terminates the consent given to the Imposter Spirit and the Negative Ego from controlling your mind. This is spiritual maturity.

It is the responsibility of each being to command the personal space and make a choice to the spiritually energetic authority, which is the Law of Consent. If no choice is made it will be made at one's consciousness frequency level combined with where one's genetic ancestry has evolved in this cycle and the quality of energetic consciousness.

HOW DO WE BECOME FREE?

Any discipline may be applied in setting spiritual goals to achieve greater Ego transcendence. You must understand that you can end the dark consequences of the Ego filter and consciousness blocking with the three factors:

- Death of the Ego and Animal nature- the psychological "I".
- Birth of the Inner Christ Spiritual being within.
- Service to others or Law of One practices as a lifestyle.

The Ego dies on rigorous creative comprehension of these larger truths. The Inner Christos Spiritual Being is born within us during our Hierogamic Union or embodied Hieros Gamos.

The service to others path is the greater sacrifice for all of humanity which is the Christos embodiment of God's eternal love.

ENQUIRE UPON BELIEFS

Motivation influences perception, perception influences beliefs, and beliefs influence actions.

In the Buddhist tradition, the three major motivation problems to overcome are greed, anger, and delusion. If these constitute or drive your motivation then your perceptions, beliefs, and actions can be twisted. Below is a good model to help us to understand ourselves better and motivate those around us.

Understanding the internal structures of Ego- the "Houses of Ego"- requires an awareness that there are three main layers. The first layer is the Chakra of the Unconsciousness Mind; the second is the Chakra of the Instinctual Mind; and the third layer is the Chakra of the Conscious Mind.

The three layers of the mind work together to serve the functions of the Ego in all human beings. Each energetic layer has separate functions yet all three layers are interconnected and directly impact each other. As we learn about the layers in the internal structure of the Ego, this clarifies the purpose of identifying what the Ego is and how it operates within us. When we understand how Ego Filters operate inside our minds, we are better equipped to heal the energetic imbalances stemming from the Negative Ego or Predator Mind.

If one's body suffered abuse or was a foetus in between lifetimes, it is recorded in one's memory storage whether or not one currently remembers consciously.

1. DIMENSION MEMORY STORAGE – UNCONSCIOUS MIND

1. Abuse
2. Trauma
3. Shock
4. Devastation

FIRST INTERNAL LAYER: This is the root layer of our unconscious mind and it functions like a hard drive for the Ego. In this hard drive is the cellular memory storage from one's entire life stream.

This means cellular memories from past lives, present lives and future lives may all be stored in this memory hard drive. These memories are not given value when they are recorded, whether one may perceive them as good or bad. The multiple memories are stored in the root hard drive of every human being.

If one's body suffered abuse or was a foetus in between lifetimes, it is recorded in one's memory storage whether or not one currently remembers consciously.

Because the planet was invaded and our individual memory and identity erased from those tragic events, human beings have four main areas of cellular memory record in their unconscious minds at varying degrees. Those four main areas are abuse, trauma, shock, and devastation.

Some people will feel these painful memories but not know what caused them or where they came from. Others suffer from shock after shutting down these memories as a coping mechanism. Others are very successful in clearing these memories through hypnosis and past life regression. Since this 1D unconscious mind controls our autonomic nervous system and autonomic bodily functions, unhealed memory trauma in these four main areas creates many kinds of physical symptoms and disease. These devastating memories have been partially described in twisted half-truths in the fall of humankind, or the Genesis story of Adam and Eve in the Bible. Starseeds and Indigos have an earth mission to heal these memories (and lifetimes) in various ways.

2. DIMENSION-WALLS OF SEPARATION INSTINCTUAL MIND

1. Unworthiness
2. Shame
3. Guilt

Lack of Trust / Self Doubt Betrayal/Abandonment Anger/Rage

Fear

SECOND INTERNAL LAYER

This is the instinctual layer of Ego. For many people it remains a part of the unconscious mind, as many ignore the cause of their instinctual drives or addictions. The first part of healing is to pay attention to drives through dedicated self-awareness.

This second layer can also be called "the pain body". It is the location where unresolved pain memories will manifest as instinctual drives within the person's Ego.

If the 1D storage memories are not identified or cleared, the pain of these memories creates "walls of separation" in the 2D layer as a pain body. The pain body further creates "walls of separation" which manifest in the Ego as seven primary mental and emotional states identified above.

These walls of separation isolate the Ego self in the person and as the person identifies with that Ego state, they become disconnected from their inner spirit. This disconnection from the inner spirit creates a wall where another part of the Ego identity may split off and hide itself.

This identity could have been created when one was a baby, a six- year-old, a teenager, or even in other timelines. This phenomenon is called "Ego sub-personalities". The personalities may be hidden behind the walls because of experienced trauma. These traumatised sub-personalities also hold a fragment of our spiritual energy. The goal of Satanic Ritual Abuse (SRA) is to create these traumatised sub-personalities which fragment the mind and spiritual body thereby causing harm to the internal energy structures of the person's aura. Currently, this is enforced en masse on the planet Earth by the NAA through the Victim/Victimiser software program.

When we are separated from our inner spirit, we are disconnected from our experience with God Source. The result is more pain, disconnection, and disease, which exacerbate the Ego walls, and perpetuates the cycle of misery. The goal of our inner spirit is to find those sub-personalities and heal them, and reclaim them as children of God, so that the spiritual light can be reintegrated and brought back into wholeness.

3. DIMENSION HOUSES OF EGO-CONSCIOUS MIND

- Addictions/Lust
- Wrath/Rage/Vengeance
- Greed/Avarice
- Envy/Jealousy
- Gluttony/Waste
- Laziness/Discouragement
- Pride/Self Importance

THIRD DIMENSIONAL LAYER:

This is the conscious mind layer of the Ego, which we perceive as a self or personality. If you pay attention to your conscious thoughts, you become aware of negative Ego thoughts as defined above by the Seven Houses of Ego. All houses of Ego are formed by making judgements of people and external circumstances. The first and second layer directly affects the third layer to the degree that the painful memory has created walls of separations and traumatised sub-personalities.

If the main areas of the walls of separation are not dismantled and sub-personalities brought for healing, these hidden influences control and manipulate the strength and power within the person's houses of Ego. Essentially, if a person is weak and in pain their walls of separation are stronger (pain body) which creates judgements that build the Houses of Ego.

In most cases, the houses are also created as a coping mechanism to deal with the harshness experienced in the 3D world. The Houses of Ego are a direct rejection of God's Spirit and repel the Christos Spirit from dwelling in one's body. If the Houses of Ego are extremely strong and the person replays its characteristic behaviour repeatedly, it builds an internal "house" which then attracts a "spirit".

For example, if a person has an addiction problem stemming from unhealed trauma and replays the addictive behaviour, a "House of Ego" is built internally. The house attracts a spirit, the same consciousness energy that will match the vibrational quality in the internal house.

The Spirit of addiction is demonic. So, as one builds a house of addiction inside their mind and body, a demonic spirit is attracted to dwell there. The laws of energetic structures state that if one has built an internal house, he or she has thus created the energetic agreement for a demonic spirit to dwell in it. This is the agreement that uninformed people make. They agree to provide a sanctuary for a demonic spirits and then later allow the predator force to use their body as a dark portal.

4. DIMENSION PERSONALITY MATRIX

The 3Dimensional Consciousness is issued in describing the limited perception of the world as being only that which is perceived in the physical. A person who limits his or her perceptions to the basic five senses would be considered as a 3Dimension person.

Such a person would not have had an awakening experience and therefore not have fully developed Higher Sensory Perception or an ability to sense energy fields and their quality.

A 3D person is usually more developed mentally than emotionally, leading them to perceive everything through their intellect. This results in dismissing Higher Sensory Perception experiences in others and in themselves.

PRIMORDIAL IMPRINTS OF SEPARATION

Originally, our blueprint came from the potential of the Twelve Strands DNA consciousness; however, during the Fall, forces of darkness ripped us apart and left us with only two strands consciousness that we came to earth with. The pain of that separation was devastating to the human collective soul.

The Guardian Host describes the core separation imprint in the human soul that now every other trauma and fear grows off as the seed fear that recorded itself into the three layers of Ego.

So after the imprint of Separation, let's say if we go back to the moment of time where consciousness came into form at this level of density, and experience polarity and duality consciousness, at these imprints planes of reality, there was a direct, at the individual level, an imprint of separation was recorded in our energetic body.

Through those imprints, our consciousness and experiences in these lower form worlds, we formed different emotions that had different energy signatures, but they were all still related to Seed Fears of the Imprint of Separation.

Going through these processes when doing holographic re-patterning, you may want to look at the primordial to go through and clear these from your holographic imprints of separation and consciousness.

The Primordial Imprints of Separation

Level 1   Shock, trauma and devastation

Level 2   Lack of trust and lack in spirit

Level 3   Betrayal and its polarity and abandonment.

          Betrayal and abandonment work together so they are listed as one.

Level 4	Fear
Level 5	Cosmic rage of cosmic anger Level 6 Unworthiness
Level 7	Shame and quilt. Apparently, that's the same vibration.
Level 8	The feeling of entrapment.

AMPLIFICATION OF FEAR POLARITIES

During the Ascension Cycle the energies of the Primordial Imprints of Separation amplify in the world scape in order for us to see them surfacing and recognise that we must shift and clear their impact upon our higher consciousness. For instance, fear and unworthiness, the primordial imprint as we list them out. They became like physical things in matter, like planes of vibration.

Suddenly, they are created in the planetary fields and within the human collective consciousness. They were manipulated into Victimiser Archetypes in the collective mind. This was the beginning of the Controllers taking advantage of this painful situation through constructing the Mind Control matrices that were installed in the earth body. So because of this trauma, we start to have these negative emotions and experiences that all stem from the original imprint of Separation that we first experienced as we went through those dark planes of existence to have this experience on earth.

This went further to main polarities of fear vibration, we could describe these imprints of separation, and these sub particular emotions that all sourced from separation. They became polarities of fear vibration on earth.

Therefore, everything is vibrating at fear level now because we are God beings and we did not know the power of our thought forms of fear and unworthiness. We created planes of existence that existed at that vibration and these are the planes that are considered hell, if we think about the Biblical and all the fundamental religious programming that talks about heaven and hell.

This is described as hell, planes of insanity. These actual planes now exist throughout the lower astral levels where souls can be trapped when they are fully vibrating at that low vibration level. Therefore, when somebody comes into consciousness into the third dimension, his or her soul wants to get beyond polarity and separation consciousness and return into the unity consciousness.

That compels us to go through these main polarities of fear vibration, to experience that fear vibration, and to go through the experience of "beingness". It entails transforming it with our inner light, moving into a higher vibration in order to transcend it. That is actually what we are doing here as a Starseed and Indigos at so many levels. Therefore, it's a different way to give clarity on a lot of what we endure as polarity integrators.

These planes of energy are like a huge group dimensional plane of space where there is just fear vibration, a plane of unworthiness, because that thought form now over so many eons of time of humans experiencing that vibration as a feeling. It actually became an existence. It formed into a plane somewhere and it became a part of the seven planes that are also known esoterically as the seven planes of the earth.

These planes of the earth are what light workers, healers and all of us that are here incarnating agree to transcend and heal. We achieve this by unifying these main polarities of fear vibration to finally unify and clear our imprints of separation so that we can move into the higher thought forms and the light codes, the language of the light of God.

Beyond fear and separation is Unity, the universal consciousness, and this is where the Law of One is founded and many beings are existing at that level. The language of light is a set of tones, vibrations, colour, instruction, and language that is all of Unity. It is all on Oneness so as we move into the language of light and are getting re-coded not only in our bodies, but on the planet Earth.

We are clearing the planes that exist from those main polarities of fear that emanated from the causation of that imprint of separation that was originally a part of what happened in the evolution of humanity. What we would refer to as the "fall of the Divine human consciousness" is when we came into density and these particular experiences were then created from our dark ignorance and confusion. This was further manipulated by unscrupulous entities we call the Controllers.

As we integrate the polarities on these lower energetic planes, each of our parallel lives is also working on this at a certain level. So, each one of us has unique sets of polarities that are expressed on multiple planes of reality through all levels we exist on.

Therefore, as we go through these cord-cutting issues, it is actually a lot more complicated than people realise. These cords are attached to these planes of existence in other timelines, and to those levels of our evolution as a light being.

We are on Earth, we are all one, and each one of us is clearing particular levels of whatever those separation imprints are for us. However, those separations and polarity imprints of fear have created miasma in our core manifestation template and this is what we need to clear.

CHAPTER THIRTEEN

SPIRITUAL MATURITY

Any disharmony should be viewed with the lens of the inner eye, looking beyond the testimony of the five outer senses. God is not the dispenser of sin, sickness and death, but the giver of every perfect gift. Imperfect conditions occur only through incorrect disharmonious use of energy by the individual himself and each individual can contribute towards reversing the situation by constructive use of energy.

To prevent darkness from manipulating your energy and influencing your body, you have to stop it in its tracks and refuse its authority or control over your being in every way. To do this, you need to identify, locate, and terminate it. It must not access your mind, emotions, body, and spirit. This takes deep conviction and strength through God and Christ's power and authority that equips you to reclaim your spiritual power and body. This calls for spiritual maturity.

WHAT IS SPIRITUAL MATURITY?

One develops this maturity through the desire to know the inner self (God Self) and healing negative Ego fears. This needs consistent practise that will develop into a sense of ethical, peaceful, compassionate, and loving behaviour in one's life.

When we achieve energetic balance between internal forces and find inner harmony, we naturally become more harmonious with all of life. Emotional maturity results in our ability to go beyond or rise above personal dramas, selfish motivations and start caring about what is happening to others.

Spiritual maturity is not religious; it has humanitarian objectives through balanced behaviours of spiritual understanding. At this level, we become aware of the group of which we are part and planetary issues facing humanity currently and in the longer term. This is group consciousness.

A spiritually mature person does not want to increase negative energy, suffering, or cause any pain. Spiritual maturity is that which identifies the true self as a spiritually energetic being and recognises that spiritual self-development is the direct cause of all that happens in the material world. Nothing manifests in the physical without a spiritual energetic causation first.

The hallmark of spiritual maturity is becoming responsible with where one puts energy and attention. Expansion of group consciousness and accumulation of spiritual knowledge through all life experiences becomes the focus of attention. Allowing your body to be the will that inspires goodness, a service to the whole and recognising that all life is interconnected is a level of spiritual maturity. It also extends to integrating the law of one practices, relationship mastery guidelines, and tools to master emotional body, mental body, and the physical body. I will discuss this in the next volume.

WHAT ARE BALANCED AND HEALTHY BEHAVIOURS?

Why is Ego-balance and emotional health a primary motivation? Beyond the drive to develop one's authentic self and actualise that self in the world, the motivation to be emotionally healthy usually stems from great personal suffering.

When we are in energetic balance with ourselves, we are in balance with our spiritual self, our hearts, and we cease to have personal turmoil or suffering. When we are emotionally healthy, we can access our spiritual self and intelligence easily. This means we understand our natural spiritual-energetic state of being in one emotional balance, inner peace, health, and connection with life.

This state is not dependent on the external outcomes and can be experienced even when others around you and the world are undergoing turmoil. To improve peace in a dysfunctional world, we may require attitudinal behaviour guidelines that help us overcome the insanity of the Archontic Deception Behaviour and their anti-life forces that abuse its mechanism.

To understand the polarity of the forces on earth and see how satanic force methods are used every day to destroy the soul of human beings, let us review both sides of the Spiritually Healthy Behaviours (GSF) and Spiritual Abuse Behaviour (AD).

Spiritually healthy behaviours naturally connect a person with God Source and Christos and are God–Sovereign-Free or GSF Behaviour. Spiritually Abusive behaviour disconnects one from God and Christ and are in the Archontic Deception Behaviour or AD Behaviours.

The goal of the discernment guideline below is to identify these spiritually abusive AD behaviours in you, others and in any external organisation where you take part and transform them through practising GSF Behaviours.

All decisions one can make from an informed position by identifying AD behaviours will increase personal discernment and energetic resonance of GSF in one's life. The only thing any person can change is themselves through their heart responses and behaviours. Change starts from within. Identify the Archontic Deception Behaviour and apply the GSF Behaviour antidote below to transform into spiritually healthy behaviour.

HEALTHY CONTROL

It is important for us to develop self-control and awareness of ourselves and have discipline over impulses in many aspects of our lives. Self- control is an important attribute of spiritual maturity, and an essential component of interconnection and feeling empathy for humanity and the planet. Achieving a healthy balance of self-discipline and self-control is an essential element of personal responsibility and accountability.

One must honour human beings and life force to achieve a healthy balance with self-discipline and control. One must consider and respect the rights and needs of others.

Loss of self-control leads to anxiety, unhappiness, anger, resentment, stress, helplessness, and even depression. Abdicating one's personal power over self-control, by acting powerless, and playing the Victim–Victimiser role, is irresponsible and self-destructive.

Keep in mind that our personal and spiritual freedom ends where other's begins. One must honour human beings and life force to achieve a healthy balance with self-discipline and control. One must consider and respect the rights and needs of others.

CHAPTER FOURTEEN

THE SPIRIT OF CHRIST

There are demonic spirits that live in the internal structures of Ego and they cause harm to our minds and bodies. People are motivated to learn how to create the internal houses for the Spirit of Christ.

As the Universal Law of Structure states, we can build our house so that the spirit can reside in it. This house must be erected in our minds and bodies, and replace Ego.

The goal of spiritual protection is to dismantle the houses of Ego, evict the demonic and predator forces, and replace them with the Houses of Christ. State your authority and intention to be of service to God and to build a strong relationship with your Inner Spiritual Light and Christos. As you devote your attention and focus on the quality of the Spirit of Christ, the Houses of Christ grow stronger. When we focus our energy and attention, the Houses return to us feelings of self-love, peace, and happiness.

The goal of spiritual protection is to dismantle the houses of Ego, evict the demonic and predator forces, and replace them with the Houses of Christ.

The Spirit of Christ gives:

- Purity
- Generosity
- Patience
- Kindness
- Discipline/Conservation
- Diligence
- Humility

Dismantle the House of Lust/Addiction: Evict the spirit of lust and addiction; call in the spirit of purity. Ask God to help you build the house of purity and live with sexual ethics in your mind and body aligned with Christ Spirit.

Dismantle the House of Wrath/Rage: Evict the spirit of wrath and rage; call in the spirit of patience. Ask God to help you build the house of patience in your mind and body aligned with Christ Spirit.

Dismantle the House of Greed/Avarice: Evict the spirit of greed and call in the spirit of generosity. Ask God to help you build the house of generosity in your mind and body aligned with Christ Spirit.

Dismantle the House of Envy/Jealousy: Evict the spirit of envy and jealousy and call in the spirit of kindness. Ask God to help you build the house of kindness in your mind and body aligned with Christ Spirit.

Dismantle the House of Gluttony/Waste: Evict the spirit of gluttony and waste and call in the spirit of discipline and conservation. Ask God to help you build the house of discipline and conservation in your mind and body aligned with Christ Spirit.

Dismantle the House of Laziness/Discouragement: Evict the spirit of laziness and discouragement and call in the spirit of diligence. Ask God to help you build the house of diligence in your mind and body aligned with Christ Spirit.

Dismantle the House of Pride/Self Importance: Evict the spirit of pride and self-importance and call in the spirit of humility. Ask God to help you build the house of humility in your mind aligned with Christ Spirit.

May we come to know the strength, protection, and peace of God on earth. Stay in the luminosity of your Avatar Christ heart path. Please be kind to yourself and each other.

PRAYERS AND MEDITATIONS

MEDITATION/PRAYER BY ST. GERMAIN

St. Germain went on to describe the method of Divine transformation: "By design of nature, our bodies are highly adaptable. Forces of high thinking and frequencies can accelerate this with our intent and voicing the following: clearing our karma, personality defects and negative thought forms and energies."

PRAYER

"I ask the Divine Cosmic Powers of the Sacred Fires from the Great Central Sun to fill me with unconditional love and consume all limitations within my world and every mistake I have ever made and clear my soul and bodies (as we have several), with the Mighty Cosmic Violet Flame.

I also call upon the Mighty Cosmic Violet Flame to consume all my discordant creations and the discordant creations of others around me. Blaze the Cosmic Violet Flame into every aspect of nature that I have harmed in any way, space, time, level, kingdom, realm, or dimension in the past, present, future, in-between and in parallel lives. I ask for the healing of all nature.

Mighty I AM Presence, charge my mind and bodies with your mighty energy, strength, courage, Divine victory and opulence. Charge every aspect of my being and world with your perfection. Bring this body into your Perfect Symmetry. Charge me with the power of the Cosmic Divine Love so I may safely and firmly move forward into the use of the greater powers without interruption.

Fill me with your invincible solution to every problem in my life. I ask for Sacred Fire Control of everything and myself in my life. I command the Divine Plan to be fulfilled in my world.

Fill me with the Ascended Master Consciousness and lead me to my ascension now.

Mighty I AM Presence, be with me this day, walk the earth with me and see that I fulfil my Divine Plan. Hold me in your heart and make me all that you are. I AM the heart and the mind of the Mighty I AM.

I call forth the Sword of Blue Flame that keeps me to cut free forever from all that I have ever sent out in this and all embodiments.

I call forth the Triple Archangel Shield to surround every aspect of my life. I ask for the Archangels Blessing in every aspect of my life.

I call forth the Triple Arcturian Shield to completely surround and protect me, my family, benevolent humans, lifeforms, places, buildings, benevolent technology, businesses, and every aspect of our lives in alignment with the Divine Plan.

I call forth the most benevolent outcome for all constructive lifeforms and call forth the Violet Flame to saturate the Earth.

Beloved Mighty I AM Presence and other Benevolent Beings of light surround and protect me, my loved ones, my home, my business, my car or my bicycle and everything in my life, with a wall of Blue Flame and the Cosmic Blue Lightning both within my Tube of Light and outside it. Let it surround me so I cannot be seen, heard, felt or smelt by anything in the dark in any of its forms, space, level, kingdom, realm or dimension in the past, present, future, in-between and in parallel lives, as a human being or in other incarnations. I call forth this protection so I can thrive in Divine Light and Love. Blaze a Ring Pass Not of Blue Flame around me for greater protection.

I call forth the Mighty Elohim, fill me and the brain of all humans and animals with the Seven-Fold Flame of Cosmic Illumination. Seal us in the Star of Gold and Divine victory; clothe us in a mantle of the Sacred Flames and the Crown of the Seven Elohim; and fan the Threefold Flame within my heart so that I stand within it.

I call forth the Angels of the Sacred Flames to walk with me this day, bring as much light, and love as possible into my life and all of nature. Bless and heal all the powers of nature and the Beings of the Elements. I call forth all the Blessings that my I AM Presence wishes to give me and I ask for the blessings of the Cosmic Beings of Divine Light and Love. For all of this, I send forth the deepest gratitude.In Christ I AM AMEN."

VEDANTA PRAYER

"Oh, Thou Infinite Holy Presence of God, the Divine Source of All Life; Hallowed be Thy Sacred Name. We bow before Thee in gratitude, praise, and thanksgiving for Thy Supreme Presence in the Universe because Thou Art I AM.

We return to Thee, Almighty One, all the power and dominion we have ever vested in any imperfect manifestation, visible or invisible, for Thou are the All-Power of the Universe and there is no other power that can act. Let Thy will be done in and through us now! Let Thy Kingdom of God Consciousness be manifest across the face of the Earth through the heart flames of all who are so blessed as to live upon it now.

Oh, Supreme Beloved One, as we lift our hearts, our vision, our Consciousness towards Thee, release the substance of Thyself to us, each according to our requirements, that as we move forward in Thy name, and upon Thy Service, we shall not be found wanting!

We ask forgiveness for all the transgressions of Thy law of love and harmony, both for ourselves and all mankind, the Forces of the Elemental Kingdom and the Kingdom of Nature. Endow us now with

Thy power and desire to forgive all who have ever caused us distress back unto the very beginning of time.

Because we are one with Thee, we fear no evil, for there is no power apart from Thee. Thou art the strength and the power by which we move ever in the path of righteousness–and now–Oh Mother of Light– show us the full glory we had with Thee in the beginning before even this world was…AMEN!"

PRAYER TO HELP MOTHER EARTH

"In the full power and authority of the beloved presence of the Mother Father God I AM, Oh Beloved Elohim of this evolving Earth, shine in all your glory of this day filled with the essence of sunlight and the aroma of pine.

To the woodland creatures in the endless forest: we reach out our energies of love and ask your forgiveness of those who ill-treat you sometimes.

To the water which flows in the rushing streams to the rivers: we ask your forgiveness for the thoughtless ways of man and their disregard for you, a living being here to help all life. Without your energies, this world would perish. We thank you for your continual flow to nourish all life. To the nature spirits which abound on Earth: we thank you for your unseen work to help all plant life grow.

To the forests, to the tall pine and seedlings just breaking through the soil, each a treasure to the world: we thank you for your willingness to support life and to grow for all humanity to use. From within this quiet place we bring energies of gratitude to each of you this day.

Oh Mother Earth, we as your grateful children stand in earnest desire to help you in any way that brings healing to you. We as your grateful children reach out our hands An offer to help you maintain a world that is free and clear. We offer this prayer to you in the Name of the Most Holy I AM Christ AMEN.

~Written by Lady Claudine, Pleiadian Goddess of Change

A GIFT FOR LIGHT-BEARERS OF THE WORLD

~ I AM a light-bearer ~
I AM a light-bearer of this shining new Earth
Clothed in God's wisdom, love, light and strength,
Sending power and peace throughout this world
Straight from the heart, making Heaven on Earth!

I AM a light-bearer of this shining new Earth Holding the One Flame, living God's power, Loving each other like sister and brother, Living in faith, peace on this Earth!

I AM a light-bearer of this shining new Earth
Like one of God's eagles soaring in strength.
I AM holding the flame, the light of God's power,
Lord Michael's Blue Flame blessing our new Earth!
AMEN!

APPLYING THE LAW OF FORGIVENESS

"Beloved Mighty Victorious Presence of God, I AM in me, Beloved Holy Christ Self, Beloved Heavenly Father and Mother, Beloved great Karmic Board, Beloved Kwan Yin, Goddess of Mercy, Beloved Lord Lanto, and the entire Spirit of the Great White Brotherhood and the World Mother, elemental life–fire, air, water and Earth!

In the name and by the power of the Presence of God which I AM, and by the Magnetic Power of the Sacred Fire vested in me, I call upon the Law of Forgiveness and the Violet Transmuting Flame for each transgression of Thy Law, each departure from Thy Sacred Covenants.

Restore in me the Christ Mind, forgive my wrongs and unjust ways, make me obedient to Thy Code, and let me walk in humility with Thee all my days.

In the name of the Father, the Mother, the Son (Divine Child), and the Holy Spirit, I decree for all whom I have ever wronged and for all who have ever wronged me:

Violet Fire, Violet Fire, Violet Fire enfold us!

Violet Fire, Violet Fire, Violet Fire hold us!

Violet Fire, Violet Fire, Violet Fire set us free!

I AM, I AM, I AM surrounded within a Pillar of Violet Flame, Violet Flame, Violet Flame.

I AM, I AM, I AM abounding in pure love for God's Great Name. I AM, I AM, I AM complete by Thy Pattern of Perfection so fair.

I AM, I AM, I AM God's radiant Flame of Love gently falling through the air.

Fall on us, fall on us, fall on us as Thy pure love.

Blaze through us, blaze through us, blaze through us within Thy flame of love.

Saturate us, saturate us, saturate us until we are your eternal instruments of Thy Pure Love. AMEN!"

In the Full Power and Authority of the Beloved Presence of God I AM"

We, the children of Earth, humbly come to the Throne of our Mother Father God to invoke into the physical plane of Earth the most intensified activity of God's Will ever manifested in the history of time.

We ask the Legions of Light serving our sweet Mother Earth to absorb this Divine Essence into every fibre of their beings and project it into the heart flames and conscious minds of every person upon and within this planet.

Blaze the Cosmic Flame of God's Will through each soul and wash away all desire for destructive activity that impedes our desire to do God's Will. Help each soul become and remain obedient to the law of harmony and be God in action at all times.

Reveal through the Flame of Illumination the Divine Purpose and Plan for each soul that we may embody spiritual courage to fulfil our plan to perfection. May the Light of God that is Eternally Victorious illuminate all humanity that we may fulfil our purpose in Divine perfection.

Let the will of God manifest in, through, and around all beings upon and within Mother Earth now and forever.

We accept Your will dear Mother Father God Manifesting now! So be it! In Your Most Holy name I AM. AMEN!"

AWAKEN EARTH!

"The Time Is Now!
Awaken! Awaken!
Remember who you are!
You are a child of God!
Sent here on a job
To clean up the Earth,
To clear out old Karma.
Rejoice for this time!
This precious opportunity!
Remember the God Light
Take it in now!"

"Reclaim the peace
And the innocence once known.
We have played the war games.
We have taken it too far!
Throw it out! What good has it done?
We have starved. We have struggled.
Shed our tears and bled our blood.
What fun we have had seeing
How miserable we could be.
So let's start a new game.
Let's see how happy we can be.
Clean up the air! Clean up the sea!
Clear out the negativity – Let it cease to be!
And give thanks for her being.

Gather up the greed, the hate, the resentment,
Gather up all the 'old stuff'.
As children of God, we no longer need it
Ignite it! Blow it up in a Flame of Violet
Transmute. Forgive. Let it go.
The old stuff is gone, needed no more.
Anchor the love of God deep within Mother Earth.
Nurture all beings upon and within her
As Divine chalices from above.
The time is now for all to know peace and prosperity.
Time to graduate and to be Divine love.
Come one and all, let us celebrate
The awakening of the light of Christos
Expanding liberty and Freedom
From 'old stuff' of illusions for all!
Together as one Divine heart
We declare God freedom on Earth!
So be it beloved I AM

DEGREE FOR ECONOMIC BALANCE

In the name of the Almighty Presence of God I AM, the Holy Christ selves of all humanity.

We summon all great beings, powers, and legions of Light concerned with the economic stability of the nations of the Planet earth to come forth now.

Beloved Archangel Michael and Lady Astrea PURIFY! (3X)

All financial institutions, all financial complexes, all activities concerned with the economic structure of the world. Remove the cause, core, effect, record and memory back to the very beginning of the time of all misuse of money or energy patterns of exchange.

Beloved Saint Germain and Beloved Lord Zadkiel Penetrate and saturate all financial structures with the most powerful activity of Violet Fire ever known! (3X)

Beloved Lord Helios and Lady Vesta

Place all control of finances and economic systems on Earth into the hands of those who serve the Light of God and dissolve all else by the Sacred Fire here and now and forever sustained

I AM.

The wise investment of energy and substance by all servers of Light who receive these benefits for the blessing of all humanity.

Beloved Angel of Restoration

Restore to us now the Divine Plan for harmonious balance in the distribution of the Earth's abundance and the limitless supply of the universe.

We gratefully accept this done in Divine Order and in accordance with God's Holy Will.

"I AM"

INVOCATION TO SOLAR PROSPERITY

As I AM that I AM now returned to Earth, I know myself as one with the Solar Fires of our Father-Mother God.

"I AM" Present in their limitless Electronic Sphere of Prosperity, endless beauty and supply of every good and perfect thing required to fulfil my Divine Plan and maintain security, happiness, joy and peace in my life.

I stand before the throne of God, expanding my solar presence, as I affirm:

I open My Flame to Solar Prosperity (3X) ... It flows through me and I AM its manifestation.

*Continue with the following insertions as well:

The Flame of my Family

The Flame of my Spiritual Activity

The Flame of my City (town or village)

The Flame of my Country

The Flame of our sweet Planet Earth

In full faith I consciously accept this manifest (3) Keep this eternally sustained and ever-expanding. Love enfolded.

So be it ... Beloved I AM"

~ From Group Avatar decrees ~

Prayer to the MOTHER FATHER God of Light by El Morya

I AM thy Holy Love, I AM thy Love for all.
I AM Alpha and Omega,
The Beginning and the Ending.
O sweet Mother Father God
In these latter days,
Speak, again, to Thy children.
Let Thy Voice be heard in us,
And through us, as we offer
Ourselves to be as living temples
For Thy Spirit.
I AM Thy Holy Love!
I AM Thy Holy Love!
Make our hearts, minds and lives
As One in Thee!
Grant to all Light-bearers
Thy peace and freedom.
That Thy Spirit might prosper within us.
Create in us a new Spirit,
Re-establish Thy heart-tie with us,
Renew in us a right spirit.
Cast us not away from Thy Presence,
But cast away the synthetic self
From our true self and Thine.
Take not Thy Holy Spirit from us,

But fill us with Thy Spirit!
Come, O God, enlighten us!
Be with us in the Ending,
As Thou was with us in the Beginning.
O Alpha and Omega,
Mother Father God!

DECREE FOR SHAMBALLA

I go within. I AM one within the Three-Fold Flames of humanity.
From the point of Oneness within all heart-flames
I invoke the assistance of all Ascended Beings concerned with The creation of the physical focus of Shamballa on Earth.
Beloved Hosts of Light, Ascended Masters, Cosmic Beings and Angelic Hosts,

The Elemental Kingdom, Ascended Master Serapis Bey,
Holy Aeolus, the Cosmic Christ, Archangel Gabriel, and Lady Hope:
As a consecrated vessel here to assist in the upliftment of all life,
In the Oneness of all humanity's Heart-flames, I call unto you:

I AM the resurrection and the life of God's perfection. For the physical focus of Shambhala and the new day, The full power of the Ascension Flame!
Raise ALL life through its action and power into perfect Christ Consciousness.

As one breath, we express our God perfection!
As one heart, we ascend all life on Earth into our Natural God Estate.
Straight from the heart, we create Heaven on Earth.
Clothed in God's wisdom, love, light and peace In gratitude, we accept the new day.

Living Flames of Cosmic Christ Purity in light expanded Thy inner presence realised, together as One Heart sustained We now step through the Golden Door into Your Glory within
SHAMBALLA, SHAMBALLA, SHAMBALLA.
Life's Resurrection accepted
As God's most Holy Name, "I AM"!

BLESSING FROM LADY QUAN YIN, GODDESS OF MERCY AND COMPASSION

May the Peace of God be on your household!

May the Love of God be in your hearts! May the Light of God be in your souls! May the wisdom of God be in your minds!

May the Strength and Vitality of God be among the members of your household!

May the health and well-being of God be manifest through the bodies, the garments which you wear!

May the Grace of God be in your worship!

May the Talents of the Genius of God be manifest through your senses!

May the fullness of victory of your own God's Plan be manifest through your souls at the close of your Earth life!

~ Beloved Quan Yin, Planetary Logos and Goddess of Mercy ~

Heart, Head and Hand Degrees

from El Morya Master El Morya

PERFECTION

I AM life of God direction Blaze
Thy Light of Truth in me. Focus
here all God's perfection, From
all discord set me free.
Make and keep me anchored ever
In the justice of Thy Plan.
I AM the presence of perfection
Living the life of God in man!

TRANSFIGURATION

I AM changing all my garments
Old ones for the bright New Day
With the Sun of Understanding
I AM shining all the way!
I AM light within, without
I AM Light is all about!
Fill me! Free me! Glorify me!
Seal me! Heal me! Purify me!
Until transfigured they describe me
I AM shining like the Son / Daughter,
I AM shining like the Sun!

RESURRECTION

I AM the Flame of Resurrection

Blazing God's pure light through me
Now I AM raising every atom
From every shadow, I AM free!
I AM the Light of God's full Presence
I AM living ever free
Now the Flame of Life Eternal
Rises up to Victory!

Peace as a Way of Life
by Lady Claudine, Goddess of Change

"I AM constantly and consciously connected to the Divine Mind of God, and I AM about the business of my God Parents.

The Peace of the Great Solar Quiet is within my being as I use my creative expressions of thought and feeling to expand the

Light of God in, through, and around me.

I AM anchoring into this world of form, the Reality of Heaven, which is the abundance and opulence of God bathing all life within the Golden Light of Peace.

When there is peace in every heart, there will be peace in every home and peace in every nation.

This peace begins with me

Here and Now

This is my Prayer,

My heart's commitment

As God's Holy Name "I AM".

AFFIRMATION OF UNITY

Beloved Micah,
Guardian Angel of the Ray of Indivisible
Unity from our God Parents;
Blaze, Blaze, Blaze The soft Blue Light from
your Cosmic Star of Unity
through us, All co-servers on the Path of Light,
And all governments, religions, races and cultures,
Until all experience the common heritage of
Spiritual Unity within God's Light and Life.
I AM the Resurrection and the Life of the ONE
spiritual family of humanity. (3X)
Beloved "I AM" AMEN

EPILOGUE

Therefore, beloved, given the facts above which I believe are the truth and light for our journey, it is only reasonable as we have entered and some are still awakening to the truth. This transition period is an ideal time for exploring and releasing forgiveness.

Forgive yourself and forgive those you have been angry with and resenting. This is not the same as allowing someone to hurt you again. You are releasing and turning your face towards increasing light and Love ahead.

Surrender to your higher essence to allow your Higher Self to take up residence within. Stop looking for answers from the outside, but look within.

The challenges we face are the stages of initiation that even Jesus, Buddha, Krishna, and many other Avatars followed. They went through these stages and set an example for us to follow. You are your own saviour, so stop expecting anyone to save you.

This book is not for entertainment but self-help spiritual principles. It notes the work of academics, experts, and practitioners in relationships.

The book is not intended to serve as a substitute for professional medical advice, examination, diagnosis, or treatment. The information is provided as is and without warranties of any kind. So readers are encouraged to use what resonates with them and discard anything they feel they are not ready to accept as we all operate from different levels of consciousness.

The intention is to inform and challenge individuals to break down walls of so-called truths and start a new foundation where relationships should be based.

As I alluded in the preface, the Holy Spirit gave me the title of this book and inspired its contents. For months, I questioned and tried to remove some topics I felt do not relate to the title of the book; I prayed about this, but ultimately, I felt compelled to keep the book, its title and contents as is.

The Holy Spirit (I AM Presence) told me that we need to establish a new foundation based on the truth for relationships. The work needs to start at individual level before trying to change or force the next person to change.

I will discuss healing in relationships, self-awareness, and Christ Consciousness in the second volume of this book. Readers who want to follow up on the topics covered in this book can refer to my website.

https://www.healingtrancendingpath.co.za
healingtrancendinpainpath@gmail.com

www.ingramcontent.com/pod-product-compliance
Lightning Source LLC
LaVergne TN
LVHW041222080426
835508LV00011B/1045